# SMALL TALK

# SMALL TALK

BY CAROLE FRÉCHETTE
TRANSLATED BY JOHN MURRELL

PLAYWRIGHTS CANADA PRESS
TORONTO

For professional or amateur production rights, please contact:
Micheline Sarrazin, Les Productions Micheline Sarrazin
6605 Chambord Street, Montreal, Quebec H2G 3C1
514.279.0258 :: info@michelinesarrazin.com

LIBRARY AND ARCHIVES CANADA CATALOGUING IN PUBLICATION
Fréchette, Carole, 1949-
[Small talk. English]
        Small talk / Carole Fréchette ; translated by John Murrell. -- First English edition.

A play.
ISBN 978-1-77091-949-5 (softcover)

        I. Murrell, John, 1945-, translator II. Title.
III.Title: Small talk. English

PS8561.R37S4913 2018        C842'.54        C2018-903307-X

Playwrights Canada Press acknowledges that we operate on land which, for thousands of years, has been the traditional territories of the Mississaugas of the New Credit, the Huron-Wendat, the Anishinaabe, Métis, and the Haudenosaunee peoples. Today, this meeting place is home to many Indigenous peoples from across Turtle Island and we are grateful to have the opportunity to work and play here.

We acknowledge the financial support of the Canada Council for the Arts—which last year invested $153 million to bring the arts to Canadians throughout the country—the Ontario Arts Council (OAC), the Ontario Media Development Corporation, and the Government of Canada for our publishing activities.

Canada Council Conseil des arts
for the Arts        du Canada

ONTARIO ARTS COUNCIL
CONSEIL DES ARTS DE L'ONTARIO
an Ontario government agency
un organisme du gouvernement de l'Ontario

Canadä

Ontario
Ontario Media Development
Corporation

The translator wishes to dedicate this book to his
admired colleague and friend, Carole Fréchette.

*Small Talk* was commissioned and produced in French by Théâtre du Peuple-Maurice Pottecher in Bussang, France, opening on July 12, 2014. It was then presented by Opéra-Théâtre de Metz Métropole on October 3 and 4, 2014. It featured the following cast and creative team:

Sébastien Amblard
Violette Chauveau
Lindsay Ginepri
Julia Vidit

And twelve actors: Patrice Caray, Estelle Delville, Thomas Fisseau, Marie-Claire Fuchs, Laétitia Gleiyse Stemer, Jean-Claude Luçon, Jean Martin, Christine Mutin, Juliette Petitjean, Odile Rose, Céline Sempiana, Céline Véron

Director: Vincent Goethals
Set Design: Jean-Pierre Demas
Costume Design: Dominique Louis
Makeup: Catherine Nicolas
Sound Design: Bernard Vallery
Lighting Design: Philippe Catalano
Dramaturg: Isabelle Lusignan
Assistant Director: Julia Vidit

NOTES

In the original French-language text of this play, the song sung by The Word-Finders (*Les mots retrouvés*) chorus is "Nous aurons," music and lyrics by Richard Desjardins. With the playwright's permission, the translator has replaced it with the ancient anonymous "Riddle Song," well-known in various versions. Here are the words for the version used in *Small Talk*:

*I gave my love a cherry that had no stone,*
*I gave my love a chicken that had no bone,*
*I gave my love a ring that had no end,*
*I gave my love a baby with no crying.*

*How can there be a cherry that has no stone?*
*How can there be a chicken that has no bone?*
*How can there be a ring that has no end?*
*How can there be a baby with no crying?*

*A cherry when it's blooming, it has no stone.*
*A chicken when it's pipping, it has no bone.*
*A ring when it's rolling, it has no end.*
*And a baby when it's sleeping has no crying.*

In the original French-language text, the song attempted by Queenie (Reine) at Julie's (Justine's) birthday party is "Gens du Pays," words and music by Gilles Vigneault. The refrain, with some word substitutions, is traditionally sung at birthday parties in Québec. With the playwright's permission, the translator has substituted the familiar "Happy Birthday Song," words and music by Mildred and Patty Hill (no longer under copyright), and, later, the traditional "For She's A Jolly Good Fellow."

## ABOUT QUEENIE'S PROBLEMS WITH LANGUAGE

Queenie is afflicted with a speech disorder resulting from cranial trauma sustained in an automobile accident. The disorder is clearly that of aphasia. The playwright has not attempted to reproduce the exact pathology of this disorder but has rather created a "theatrical version" of it (which the translator has attempted to reproduce in English). Queenie's syntax is intact; it is vocabulary which fails her. She is not aware of her mistaken or invented words. From time to time, she happens upon the correct word, but more frequently her choices are nearly indecipherable by others. Frequently, there is an "echo" of the correct word in the word Queenie uses, but not always. For example, in the original French-language version of the play, Queenie may say "pomme" when she means "donne"; but, at another time, she may replace "donne" with a different word. Her problem is, in fact, twofold: she can no longer find the correct words, and she can no longer understand what is said to her. In the play, she may seem to understand what Julie or Charlie say to her, but a careful reading will reveal that she only understands them when they are using the simplest of phrases, and especially when these are accompanied by explanatory gestures. When Julie tries to explain to her mother that she (Julie) must change, she knows that Queenie does not understand. Julie attempts to find a gesture which will convey the concept of change itself, but, since the concept is an abstract one, such a gesture is unclear, and Queenie does not grasp its meaning. On the other hand, when Julie says, "I have to go," and points to her watch, Queenie understands at once.

It may seem strange that others persist in conversing with someone who can rarely if ever understand or reply understandably, but this is accepted practice with victims of aphasia. One speaks to them, knowing that 90% of what one says will not be understood. One speaks in order to establish, in spite of everything, a line of communication, seizing upon the small victories of a communicative gesture, effective mimicry, a shared smile of recognition.

## CHARACTERS

Julie
Timothy
Narrator

Queenie, Julie's mother
Charlie, Julie's brother
Earl, Julie's father
Kristin, Earl's second wife
Galina, Charlie's girlfriend

Sheila, Julie's co-worker
Diane, likewise

Emily Goodman, an old schoolmate of Julie's

Coach, a woman who appears on the website "Ten Easy Steps To Better Chatting"
Fran, appears on the same website
John, likewise

George, singer in The Word-Finders, an amateur chorus
Janet, likewise
Ernie, likewise
Larry, likewise
Anita, conductor of The Word-Finders chorus

Rachel, participant in a workshop called "Communicating With Others"
Ian, likewise
Sylvia, likewise
Kevin, likewise
Marvin, likewise
Marguerite, leader of the "Communicating With Others" workshop

Luke, a television director

# I. IS THIS THE PLACE?

NARRATOR: Monday afternoon, on a wide thoroughfare in an industrial park. A bus shelter. Concrete floor. Plexiglas walls. On the back wall, a tattered poster offers a self-improvement course. Only a few words are legible: "Communicating With Others"—or maybe "Communicating With Otters"? Hard to be sure. At the bottom are little detachable slips of paper with a telephone number. Across the poster somebody's written "Fuck You" in ink. It's three p.m. There's not much traffic. The workers are at work. Nobody else has any reason to be here. Behind the bus shelter, a building from the seventies, a cube of glass and concrete. A brass plaque beside the front door says "Lowell Laboratories." A bus comes by. It stops in front of the shelter. A young man gets off. He carries a large gym bag. The bus leaves. The young man watches it go. He looks around at the street, the buildings, the parking lots. He enters the bus shelter. He sits on the concrete bench. This is Timothy.

TIMOTHY: Is this the place?
Ugly enough, isn't it?
It took me an hour to get here. Had to change buses twice.
You say to me: "You didn't need to go so far. There's ugliness everywhere."
Sure, but we specified "industrial ugliness."
Concrete and asphalt ugliness. No trees and no passersby.
Ugly, soulless buildings in an industrial desert.
I see the tattered poster.
I feel an impulse.
"Go with your impulse, Timothy." Isn't that what you say to me?
I see the word "Laboratories" on the building. In school, I hated "Lab Day."

The smell made me heartsick.

You realize there are thousands of people who work here?

They arrive at nine o'clock. They spend the day bent over their microscopes. For lunch, they warm up yesterday's spaghetti in the microwave. At five o'clock, they go home. They eat chicken nuggets in front of the TV.

Isn't that "ugliness"?

I mean, all of that.

You don't know. You don't give a shit.

You think I'm just rambling, not really doing anything.

Not true.

I'm doing something.

I'm searching.

I got up at noon. I phoned work. I told them, "I'm not coming in tonight." The boss shouted, "How're you going to do me like that? The bar will be packed!"

I looked at a city map and selected a route. I got ready. I brought my gym bag.

You think that's nothing?

That's not nothing.

So now I'm here, but I'm still not sure.

How can I be sure?

Is this the place?

## 2. HOW'S IT GOING?

NARRATOR: Time passes. Two or three buses stop at the shelter. People get off. They don't notice the young man on the concrete bench and he doesn't notice them. Nobody else enters the shelter. Then he stands, picks up his bag, and leaves. It's five p.m. now. The employees of Lowell Laboratories begin to emerge. A line of cars exits the parking lot. A woman enters the bus shelter. She sits in front of the tattered poster. She looks at her watch. She waits. A few minutes later, a somewhat younger woman comes along and stops at the entrance to the shelter. This is Julie.

JULIE: Hi.

SHEILA: Hi.

*Silence.*

JULIE: Kind of chilly.

SHEILA: Are you cold?

JULIE: Uh . . . no. They say it's going to warm up tomorrow.

SHEILA: Do they? I don't know.

*Pause.*

JULIE: Taking its time.

SHEILA: What?

JULIE: The bus.

SHEILA: It'll be here at five fifteen, same as always. Since when do you take the thirty-five?

JULIE: What?

SHEILA: You don't take the thirty-five. Don't you usually walk home?

JULIE: I . . . I don't know.

SHEILA: Don't you live around here somewhere?

JULIE: No. I mean "Yes." But I was just going to—

SHEILA: Diane says you do. I don't know how she knows. She must've been snooping through your file.

JULIE: I don't know. But . . . What about you, Sheila? How's it going?

SHEILA: You'd never just mention that to Diane, would you?

JULIE: What?

SHEILA: That you live around here somewhere.

JULIE: No. Probably not. I don't talk to Diane much.

SHEILA: That's for sure. You don't talk to Diane much, or to Muhammad, or to Melanie, or to Mr. Dexter, or to the janitor, or to the mailroom boy, or to me. You don't talk to anybody much.

JULIE: No, but . . . I'm talking to you now. I . . . Did you have a good day, Sheila?

SHEILA: Exactly like yours, Julie. I did the same stuff you did, all day long.

*Pause.*

JULIE: Did you see the coverage of the floods yesterday?

SHEILA: What floods?

JULIE: All those people climbing up onto their roofs.

SHEILA: Where was that?

JULIE: Pakistan. No, Sri Lanka. I don't remember.

SHEILA: Can I ask you something?

JULIE: Of course.

SHEILA: Where do you go at lunchtime? And for coffee breaks? You disappear. Ever since you started work at the lab, three years ago, you just disappear. Everybody wonders where you go.

**JULIE:** Right. Listen, I have to . . . I've got to go. I forgot. I'm meeting somebody. Sorry.

*JULIE escapes.*

## 3. TEN EASY STEPS TO BETTER CHATTING

**NARRATOR:** A few hours later, in the kitchen of a no-frills second-storey apartment, twenty minutes by foot from Lowell Laboratories. Three rooms and bath, very tidy. Low ceilings, sliding windows, a sliding door onto a balcony shared with the apartment next door. On the kitchen table, a computer. On the computer screen, a smiling woman. This is the coach for "Ten Easy Steps To Better Chatting."

**COACH:** So you had a little setback? Not to worry. You took the first step, that's what counts. You didn't die of it, did you? Now then: What exactly happened? Touch "Enter" when I get to the right answer.
"You didn't know how to kick off the conversation"?
"You knew how to kick it off, but not how to keep it going"?
"You introduced several topics but were unable to build on them"?
"You panicked"?

**JULIE:** Enter. Enter. Enter.

**COACH:** That's okay. It was your first time. A setback is never pleasant, but it's best to find the cause right away. Then you can try again. Was the person you selected for conversation someone known to you socially?

**JULIE:** Enter.

**COACH:** Fine. It's good to start with someone you know. Excellent. Now, let us consider precisely what happened. In order to move forward, we must dissect the problem.

**JULIE:** What happened is that I'm hopeless.

COACH: Touch "Enter" to respond "Yes." Did you initiate the conversation?

JULIE: Enter.

COACH: What topic did you introduce? Touch "Enter" when I get to the right answer.
"The weather"?
"The—"

JULIE: Enter.

COACH: That's a great way to begin. Some may say the weather is banal, but you can always build on banality. Do not exclude mundane topics, sometimes called "small talk." Every conversation starts there. Placing one word pebble on top of another, we construct a lofty dialogue. Let us return to your recent experience. Touch "Enter" when I get to the right answer.
"The other person didn't warm to your topic"?
"He or she warmed to your topic, but you didn't know how to keep it going"?

JULIE: What does "warmed to my topic" mean?

COACH: Touch "Enter" when I get to the right answer.

JULIE: She said, "Are you cold?" with her usual cold look. I answered, "Uh . . . no," with my usual stupidity.

COACH: Touch "Enter" when I get to the right answer.

    *Pause.*

You can't decide where to go from here? Not to worry. We'll cover all this material again in Lesson Two. Meanwhile, if you wish, you may click on "Dialogue" and then on "Weather." Here you will view a brief conversation demonstrating how to keep this simple topic going. Remember: it's only an example. It's up to you to find the right words for your particular circumstances. Conversation is improvisation. To proceed, click on "Dialogue."

JULIE: Dialogue. Weather. Enter.

*FRAN and JOHN appear on the computer screen, in an office setting.*

FRAN: Hi, John.

JOHN: Hi.

FRAN: Lousy weather today.

JOHN: Mmm.

FRAN: Supposed to continue for several days.

JOHN: Mmm.

FRAN: The rain always makes me nostalgic. How about you?

JOHN: Not especially.

FRAN: It makes me think about those rainy days at the beach during my summer holidays. I got so bored. But I'll bet you liked rainy days when you were a kid.

JOHN: Don't remember.

FRAN: I'll bet you liked splashing around in the puddles.

JOHN: Yeah, I did like that.

FRAN: Splashing around by yourself?

JOHN: No, with my brother. We had contests to see who could make the biggest splash.

FRAN: You have a brother?

JOHN: Yes. A twin brother.

FRAN: Really? That's interesting. I had no idea. An identical twin?

JOHN: Identical. When we were kids everybody got us mixed up.

FRAN: But not now?

JOHN: Now we look different. He has a beard and long hair.

FRAN: You must be really close.

JOHN: Well, yes and no. He lives in Australia.

FRAN: Australia! I've dreamed of Australia. Do you go there often? I'd love to visit Australia. Especially the Great Barrier Reef.

JOHN: I've been diving in the Great Barrier Reef. It was amazing. I saw a giant jellyfish.

FRAN: A giant jellyfish? Tell me all about it. I'm so into jellyfish.

JOHN: Oops! I think they're calling us. The meeting's about to start up again. Nice talking to you, Fran.

FRAN: Nice talking to you, John.

COACH: You see how a banal topic like the weather can take you quite far. All the way to Australia! Did you notice how John kept shutting down the conversation at first? But Fran was not discouraged. She found a way to shift the conversation into a more personal gear. Encourage the other person to talk about himself or herself. That's an important key to better chatting. Would you like to discover how to improvise more smoothly? It's all a matter of training. Click on "Training," then on "Weather," then on—

*JULIE turns off her computer.*

## 4. SOLILOQUY

**NARRATOR:** Julie sits staring at her computer for a long time. Then she restarts it. She carefully rereads the list of "Ten Easy Steps To Better Chatting."
Step One: Getting Started: Rely on simple topics.
Step Two: Focus On The Other Person: Make him or her feel important.
Step Three: The Art Of The Restart: Know how to bounce back.
Step Four: Body Language: An essential component.
Step Five: Three-Way Conversations: The dynamics of complex interaction.
Step Six: Anecdotes: Spicing up the small talk.
Step Seven: Unforeseen Encounters: How to avoid panic.
Step Eight: The Art Of Closure: How to terminate naturally.
Step Nine: Cocktails, Celebrations, Getting A Groove On: The ultimate challenge.
Step Ten: The Key To Success: Being yourself.

All of a sudden, Julie feels exhausted. She moves to the living room. A sofa, a TV, a coffee table. Van Gogh prints on the walls: *Irises, Starry Night*. In one corner, a straight-backed chair and a floor lamp.

*JULIE sits in the chair. She turns on the lamp.*

**JULIE:** Did you ever go to Australia, Sheila, to visit your identical twin sister who used to splash around with you in the puddles? You don't have a twin sister, Sheila? Too bad. They say a twin can read your mind. She understands you immediately, no need to initiate, or to restart, or to terminate. She knows all about you, even your most secret secrets. She knows that you feel lonely and that you're tired of this constant soliloquy. "Soliloquy": that's my brother's word, Sheila. He went to theatre school. He says that talking to yourself in a spotlight is called a soliloquy. He says that all actors love those. He says they're intoxicating. Once you've tasted soliloquy, you never want to stop. And that's true. It starts out simply enough. One night, you speak a few words into the silence—some things you saw that day, some thoughts you had. And suddenly you feel better. The next day, you return to the same chair, but now you stay longer. All you have to do is open your mouth and out they come—observations, ideas, your views on the meaning of life. Sometimes you get confused, but so what? You soliloquize more and more frequently. You turn off the TV, you sit down right after supper, you start talking, and it is truly intoxicating—you're swept away in the wave, and you feel . . . What? Intensely alive maybe. But, afterwards, there's a bitter taste in your mouth. You feel ridiculous, ashamed. You tell yourself you've got to stop. The more words you scatter around your living room, the fewer words you have to exchange with other people, with somebody you bump into at five o'clock in the bus shelter.

*The telephone rings.* JULIE *continues her soliloquy while it goes on ringing.*

You tell yourself, "I must learn to say, 'Hi, Sheila, how's it going? Your holiday, your kids, your family?' and 'Me? Oh, I'm doing okay, but I'd really love to go to Australia. I hear they've got jellyfish down there' . . . "

*The answering machine is heard, a mechanized voice, with* JULIE *speaking her own name at the appropriate time:*

ANSWERING MACHINE: Your call has been forwarded to an automated voice-messaging system. "Julie" is not currently available. At the tone, please record your message.

CHARLIE: *(on the machine)* Hi, baby sister. Out at another wild party? That's a joke. I'm sure you're there, watching your big brother on the PVR. That's also a joke. I know you don't spend your evenings watching my show. But today you really missed something. There was this explosion of laughter right in the middle of the game. The contestants, the audience, everybody was laughing so hard they cried. They couldn't stop. It's trending on the Internet right now if you want to check it out. But that's not why I'm calling. I need to talk to you. But, okay, you're not answering. Why don't you ever answer? Are you and some guy you picked up screwing like wild animals? That's a joke! Okay. I'll let you get on with it. Call me back, okay?

JULIE: My brother's on TV, Sheila. He aspired to play the great roles in the great plays, but, right after he got out of theatre school, he auditioned to host a prime-time game show. They said he was a natural and hired him immediately. He says entertaining people is just as important as delivering soliloquies on the meaning of life.

*She turns off the lamp.*

## 5. WORKING THE EGGS INTO THE DOUGH

NARRATOR: The following day. Twelve thirty p.m. In another building, not far from Julie's. Queenie's apartment. Same low ceilings, same sliding windows. Same sliding door onto a tiny balcony. Every room crammed to overflowing with knick-knacks, curios, photos, pillows, lace doilies, plastic bouquets. Not one square inch unoccupied. In the living room, on the coffee table, tons of little jars and bottles: creams, powders, gels, perfumes.

JULIE: Did Mrs. Landau bring you all these free samples? Nice of her. But don't you think you've got enough for a while?

*QUEENIE takes a little jar from the table, opens it, and holds it out to JULIE.*

QUEENIE: Snip.

JULIE: Smells good. Lily of the valley, isn't it? Lily of the valley?

QUEENIE: Right. Billy. Snips of billy. Mice, eh?

JULIE: "Lily," Mom.

QUEENIE: I know, I know: billy.

*Holding out another jar:*

Snip up this. Snip, snip. You muff it? Let me sneer some, Charlotte.

JULIE: I'm "Julie," Mom. Charlotte was your sister. Your sister who died when you were a little girl. I'm Julie, and you are Queenie. Say it. You got it almost right last week.

*Pointing to her mother and then herself:*

Queenie and Julie.

QUEENIE: I know, Tina and Sukie. Now I sneer you some. You muff this.

*She dabs her finger in the cream and begins to rub it into JULIE's face.*

Mee? Dee? So so good. Snips the seemark. Seemark and brylick.

JULIE: Listen, Mom. I need to tell you—

QUEENIE: Brylick, you muff so, right? Mrs. Panda says it's all blue. It's the fadest pad, brylick and—

JULIE: There's no such thing as "brylick," Mom. I don't know what you're trying to tell me.

*QUEENIE takes another cream and begins rubbing it into JULIE's hands.*

QUEENIE: This is good. Snips mackunder. So nitch. It rakes the bands off. Nice, eh? Mackunder with mint of mime.

*JULIE takes the hand cream from QUEENIE, lifts it to her nose, and sniffs it, then makes a face.*

JULIE: Lavender. You know I don't like lavender.

QUEENIE: I'm living it. You muff, so it's a crescent.

*She gives JULIE the jar.*

JULIE: Thanks, Mom. But listen now. Just for a minute, okay? I've decided I have to change. I . . . . How can I explain?

*JULIE tries to mime the word "change." She indicates herself, gestures to indicate moving in one direction, then suddenly switches to move in the opposite direction.*

I have to change *me*. I can't go on sitting by myself, talking to myself. No more soliloquies. "Soliloquy": that's Charlie's word. Remember? Charlie.

QUEENIE: Paul?

JULIE: No. Paul was your dad. Charlie's my brother.

*JULIE gestures to indicate someone taller than she is.*

Charlie.

QUEENIE: Paulie? My Paulie, he's a pilot. You crash his snow yestern? His crow? He starts to calf—calf!—then everypotty calfs, and Paulie, my Paulie, he rubbles up, this like, and calfs till he dries.

*QUEENIE laughs. She doubles up to show how CHARLIE was laughing during his show. She wipes away imaginary tears to show how CHARLIE laughed until he cried.*

JULIE: You mean his show yesterday? I know, I heard it was really funny. But just listen to me, please. Mom, I have to change. I found a website that provides the basic training. I don't know how to explain. It's pretty expensive, but I don't give a damn. I need to change. I want to fit in.

*She tries to explain with gestures but can't.*

Fit in. Fit in with others. I don't know how to . . . Like immigrants fitting into our society. No, that's too complicated. Fitting in. Working myself in. Like working eggs into the dough.

*She mimes breaking eggs, then working them into a dough.*

I have to work myself in, like the eggs, until the dough is smooth and has no lumps.

*QUEENIE imitates JULIE's gestures.*

QUEENIE: What's it? Sexercise?

JULIE: I need to work myself in. Into the group. In with the others. Understand? No. You don't. Not a word. I know you don't.

QUEENIE: What you selling her, Charlotte?

JULIE: I can't have lunch with you tomorrow, because I need to have lunch with the others, at the lab. To work myself in. I'm not going to hide in the warehouse anymore every time there's a coffee break. Understand?

QUEENIE: Okay, okay. You come. I'll pee here.

JULIE: No. You don't get it. I have to go now. I'm late.

*JULIE holds up her watch and indicates that it's time for her to go.*

QUEENIE: Okay, I go, I go. You peeve. Galaways you peeve. You peeve and I die. I die.

JULIE: You cry? Is that what you mean? You *cry*?

*JULIE gestures to indicate tears flowing down her cheeks.*

QUEENIE: I dry. It's mad. My fife is mad.

JULIE: I know you want me to stay. But I can't. I have to go back to work, Mom.

*She kisses QUEENIE on the cheek.*

QUEENIE: Muff you so, my earl.

JULIE: I'm Julie, Mom. Earl is my dad and you don't love him at all. I've got to go. I'll see you Thursday night. For the chorus. The chorus.

*She sings:*

"I gave my love a cherry that had no stone . . . "

QUEENIE: I know, I know, the horse. Don't mike the horse. Out a moon, bad bad dingers.

JULIE: The chorus is good for you. You know it is. For finding your words. See you Thursday, Mom. But not for lunch tomorrow. Understand? Of course you don't. I'm sorry.

*JULIE leaves.*

## 6. THE COURAGE OF CHIHUAHUAS

NARRATOR: The following day. The employees' lunch room at Lowell Laboratories. A small windowless space in the basement. Fluorescent lighting. Faded travel posters on the walls. A microwave, a fridge. A woman prepares to warm up last night's spaghetti.

JULIE: *(coming in shyly)* Hi.

*She starts again, with greater confidence.*

Hi, Diane.

DIANE: Julie? Are you having lunch here?

JULIE: I . . . I read somewhere that the courage of chihuahuas is inversely proportional to their size. Is that true?

DIANE: What?

JULIE: I'll bet Canasta is courageous. I'll bet she's twice as brave as she is big. Or twice as small as she is brave!

DIANE: Sorry, I don't know what you're talking about.

JULIE: Don't you have a dog?

*SHEILA appears in the doorway.*

SHEILA: Diane doesn't have a chihuahua. She has a poodacock.

DIANE: It's a *cockapoo*, Sheila. And her name's Mascara.

JULIE: Oh, right. Mascara. Sorry. I got it all wrong. It's because of my mother.

DIANE: Your mother?

JULIE: She can't talk anymore, and I spend so much time with her—

DIANE: Your mother's a mute?

JULIE: No. She speaks, but she's lost the words. I mean, she still has them, but she can't find the right ones. They just tumble out, any old way. Once in a while she gets it right, but most of the time—

SHEILA: They "tumble out, any old way"?

JULIE: I . . . You're . . . Don't you go to the gym on Wednesdays?

SHEILA: Not today. Our trainer's on vacation.

DIANE: Where'd you read that, Julie?

JULIE: What?

DIANE: About chihuahuas.

JULIE: HousePets-dot-com.

SHEILA: Are you planning to buy a dog?

DIANE: If you're shopping for a dog, I can tell you that cockapoos are wonderfully caring animals. They can read your mind. Yesterday when I got home, I was so depressed, and Mascara picked up on it right away.

SHEILA: So she ran you a nice hot bath and brought you a glass of wine.

DIANE: Enough with the sarcasm. I know you don't like dogs.

SHEILA: Those fuzzy little objects that people push around in strollers aren't dogs. They're Barbie dolls with fangs.

DIANE: Go ahead and laugh. At least I have somebody in my life. I tell her everything.

SHEILA: And does she respond?

DIANE: Does your TV respond?

SHEILA: What do you mean by that?

DIANE: Does it jump into your lap? Does it cuddle up and keep you warm? Does it look at you with big, soft eyes?

SHEILA: No, my TV doesn't jump into my lap. And I don't kid myself that I'm having a conversation with it. I recognize that I'm all alone.

*An uneasy silence.*

DIANE: So you're interested in chihuahuas, Julie?

JULIE: I'm interested in courage.

DIANE: In "*courage*"?

JULIE: I . . . What time is it? Twelve thirty. I have to make a phone call. Excuse me.

DIANE: You didn't eat anything.

JULIE: I have to go.

*She leaves.*

SHEILA: *(calling after her)* You forgot your phone!

## 7. TEN EASY STEPS TO BETTER CHATTING: LESSON TWO

NARRATOR: Julie's kitchen. The table is littered with what's left of supper: a half-eaten lamb chop, an untouched salad, dessert still in the plastic wrap. Nearly eight o'clock. It's unusual that Julie hasn't washed the dishes and put them away. She sits there for a long time, staring into the mess. She pushes the dirty dishes aside and plunks her laptop down among bits of food. She stares at the smile on the coach's face, frozen on the screen, then decides to touch "Enter." .

COACH: In Lesson One, we saw how easy it is, by introducing every-day topics, to lead the other person to talking about himself or herself. Every human being loves to do this. Now we're going to learn a few little tricks to help you make the other person feel important. Think of someone you know. Try to recall his or her major interests. Here are some possible major interests:
"Gardening"
"Movies"
"Books"
"Swimming"
"Pets"

JULIE: Enter.

COACH: You've chosen "Pets." Very good. Now you need to think up three questions about the other person's pet. Does that seem too hard? Don't worry, I will help you. Touch "Enter" to continue.

JULIE: I did all that. I went to HousePets-dot-com. I learned all about chihuahuas. I thought up three questions.

COACH: Touch "Enter" to continue.

JULIE: I wrote my questions down. I memorized them. I was going to start with the easiest one: "How old is your chihuahua, Diane?" But then I messed it all up.

COACH: Touch "Enter" to continue.

JULIE: Then Sheila came in, which wasn't supposed to happen, because I haven't worked up to "Three-Way Conversations" yet. And then I said, "I'm interested in courage." In "*courage*"! What made me say that?

COACH: Touch "Enter" to continue.

*JULIE shuts down her computer.*


8 . IF I HAD A COCKAPOO


*JULIE appears in the doorway to her living room. She stares at the straight-backed chair. She approaches it, but then moves away. She approaches it again. Finally, she sits in it and turns on the floor lamp.*

JULIE: If I had a cockapoo, it would sit at my feet. We would chat. I would ask it, "How was your day, Mr. or Ms. Cockapoo? Myself, I found three cancers. Only three, out of all the samples I analyzed. It's odd, but I was elated by this discovery. A small victory over the absurd. If we fail to find cancer cells, what's the point of our work? I go about my job mechanically, then all of a sudden I see that particular design. Like a little embryo of death inside someone's life, and suddenly my heart is racing, as though I'd found a gold nugget inside a heap of rubble. Sometimes I stop and I think about the person this tiny morsel of flesh belongs to. Not supposed to do that, I know. One of the first things they taught me on the job. But today I stopped, and I thought about that woman when she visits her doctor. She feels hot and she trembles a little, and the doctor says, 'I'm afraid it's not good news,' and the woman's heart is about to explode, and the doctor says, 'We're going to fight this thing together, aren't we?' but she hears nothing, because of the screaming inside her head. I thought of her and I felt like crying. But maybe it was for my own life. Don't we always cry for ourselves? You watch a disaster on TV and you cry because you imagine yourself on the roof of your own flooded home. What do you think about that, Mr. or Ms. Cockapoo?" He or she looks at me and says nothing. Because it's only a soliloquy in disguise. Long soliloquies from me, interrupted by little whimpers from him or her. Stop it, Julie. That's not conversation, not sharing, not fitting in. That's not courage and you know it. Courage is twice as big as you are.

*She turns off the lamp.*

## 9. IS THIS THE PLACE?

NARRATOR: Later that same evening. A vacant lot. The sort of place where nasty things happen in a gangster movie. Wrecked autobodies, scrap iron, drainpipes, broken bottles, plastic bags which flap in the wind. All surrounded by an abused wire fence. With a gaping hole in it. A young man crawls through the hole. It's Timothy. He starts a fire in a rusty barrel. He takes a notepad out of his pocket. He writes on the scraps of paper. He throws them into the fire.

TIMOTHY: The word "accomplish."
The word "succeed."
The word "somebody."

As in, "To become somebody."
The word "win."
As in, "Win-win."
The word "brilliant."
As in, "The future."
"Matter."
As in, "Doing something that matters."
"Realize."
"Potential."
As in, "Realize your fucking potential."
"Do it."

We came here, remember?
You brought me here.
We drank a bottle of tequila.
We made lists.
We threw them into the fire.
A list of the ugliest places.
A list of the most ridiculous people we know.
We laughed like idiots.
We stuck our hands in the fire.
We took an oath.

This morning, I said to myself: "It has to be a ritual."
I thought of this place.
Of that night.
It was magic.
We were possessed.
But not now.
Now it's not magic.
I'm just drunk.
I'm just heartsick.

All the same, this could be the place.
A young man in a vacant lot surrounded by the world's garbage.
You think that's trite.
You say to me: "That's not honest."

You say to me: "Go with your impulse."
What impulse?
Do I even have impulses?

*Pause.*

The word "courage."
As in, "Show them your courage, kid."
"Forget."
As in, "Forget it."
Not the girl for you.
A weird girl.
A trashy girl.
The word "life."
As in, "Aw, fuck it."


## 10. THE WORD-FINDERS, AN AMATEUR CHORUS

NARRATOR: It's Thursday now. Chorus day. This morning, Julie wanted to try out "Step Three: The Art Of The Restart" with her neighbour across the hall. She walked right up to her and said, "How are you doing today, Mrs. Khoury?" Her neighbour was so pleased to be asked that she talked about how sick she is for seven minutes non-stop, then her husband called her, and Julie didn't have a chance to restart. She stood there at the door for a long time, simultaneously frustrated and relieved, then she went to work. Now it's nighttime. Julie and Queenie take a bus to the hall where the amateur chorus called The Word-Finders rehearses. They arrive in front of the old stone building. A former elementary school converted into a community centre.

JULIE: Go ahead, Mom. I'll just nip around the corner for a coffee.

QUEENIE: *(hanging onto her)* Play. Play with nee. Don't mike the horse.

JULIE: Mom, you know I don't like waiting around.

QUEENIE: Play. Peach play.

JULIE: You don't need me. The others will be coming. You'll get to sing. You don't need me to help you sing.

QUEENIE: You leap. Malaways you leap.

*JULIE tries to explain, miming the words awkwardly.*

JULIE: I'll nip around the corner for a coffee, like every Thursday. When you're through, you come find me, and we'll order chocolate ice cream. Like always.

*JULIE starts to leave. QUEENIE hangs onto her.*

QUEENIE: No, no, no. Don't leap. Play for a mint.

JULIE: What is it? What's wrong?

QUEENIE: You don't give me.

JULIE: Give you? What? You've got your music. You've got your glasses. You've got everything you need.

QUEENIE: You don't give. Don't give me for.

JULIE: What do you need? Money? You don't need money tonight, but okay, here's some money.

*She takes money from her bag, offers it to her mother, but QUEENIE won't take it.*

QUEENIE: No. No. No. It's no. Not fat. I don't mask. Give. Give me for.

JULIE: I don't understand, Mom. The others will be coming, and I'd rather not talk to them. We agreed about that, remember? So I'm going, okay?

*GEORGE, a man in his fifties, comes in.*

GEORGE: *(to QUEENIE)* Hello, DeeDee. How's flings?

*(to JULIE)* Hello. I'm George. You blue to the horse?

JULIE: No, I—

QUEENIE: *(to GEORGE)* Hi. Hi, Paul. I want to interview my mom. My mother Sukie.

JULIE: I'm Queenie's daughter. My name's Julie.

GEORGE: Oh! Great. Excellent. Delighted. Mice feather, eh?

QUEENIE: Mom's going to ching with um. She mikes it. Yes, Charlotte? You mike a ching?

*She tries to drag JULIE inside.*

GEORGE: Sure. Come on in. It'll sneer up the gloop. Don't be shine. *Shy.*

JULIE: It's not that. I'm not shy. Give me a kiss, Mom. I'll be just around the—

QUEENIE: Paulie, bake her stray. She won't whistle to me.

*JANET, a woman in her forties, comes in. She makes a real effort to find the right words.*

JANET: Hello. Queenie.

*(to JULIE)* Hello. Are . . . you . . . noon? No. Wait. Are you . . . nude? New! Yes! Are you *new*? I'm Janet.

QUEENIE: *(to JANET)* Hi, Cindy. I intersluice Josie, my cousin.

JULIE: I'm her daughter, Julie.

JANET: *(to QUEENIE)* You've got a rotter. *Daughter.* Lovely.

JULIE: I was just going.

QUEENIE: She came to thing. She doves a thing.

> *Two more members of THE WORD-FINDERS, ERNIE and LARRY, arrive.*

ERNIE: Evening, everydoddy.

QUEENIE: Hi. Hello. I want to extrodupe my bum. She haunts to swing with us.

ERNIE: Hi. How are you?

LARRY: You book a-same. Same ties. Same south. You her mother? Come to ming? Great.

ERNIE: Me, I got the bad mold. I'm gonna be coarse.

> *He coughs.*

LARRY: Bad hold? Me too. And a tore coat.

> *JULIE tries to slip away, but is prevented by the arrival of ANITA, conductor of THE WORD-FINDERS. Greetings are exchanged.*

ANITA: Good evening, everyone. Hi. How's it going?

GEORGE: Mine. All mine.

ANITA: Julie, I didn't see you! You're welcome to stay, if you like. You won't bother me.

JULIE: Thanks, but I ought to—

LARRY: Hi, Adida. I meed to—

ANITA: It's "Anita," Larry. Say "Anita."

LARRY: *(concentrating)* Anita. Got a bit of a more tote.

*He coughs.*

ERNIE: Me too. Bad gold. Gonna be norse.

*He coughs.*

ANITA: That's okay. Just don't force the voice. Right? Your voice. Don't push it. Understand?

ERNIE: I moo. I blunder and.

LARRY: I'll thing wyattly.

ANITA: We should get started. Find your places, please. Sure you don't want to sing with us, Julie?

JULIE: No, I really can't!

*She starts out.*

QUEENIE: *(to JULIE)* Don't! Don't leap! Play. Bake her play, Lolita.

ANITA: Julie, wait! What's the problem?

*QUEENIE gestures for JULIE to come back.*

ERNIE: Stay. You flit in a day.

JANET: Yes, please. Ching, ding—sing with bus. With gus. With us!

*JANET claps her hands. GEORGE joins in the clapping. Then the others join in too.*

QUEENIE: You don't give. Don't give me.

JULIE: Give you *what*, Mom? Give you my jacket? Give you my watch? Give you my life?

QUEENIE: You get for me. Malaways, malaways, you get it for. You don't give.

ANITA: What's wrong, Queenie?

QUEENIE: She won't give. Won't give it, so I die.

ANITA: Wait. You're going too fast. Try again.

JULIE: I never know what she wants. It's not the end of the world. She's been like this for the past four years. I'm used to it. In a little while she'll relax.

ANITA: Wait.

JULIE: She knows I'll be just around the corner.

ANITA: Wait. Queenie, what are you trying to say?

QUEENIE: She don't give me.

ANITA: Give? You mean "give," like this?

*ANITA mimes giving.*

QUEENIE: No, no. She doze. She throws. From me.

ANITA: Throws you? Throws you away, like the trash?

QUEENIE: No.

*(to JULIE)* You don't give. Don't give nor. Don't give for. Give.

ANITA: For. Give. She doesn't *forgive*? Is that what you mean, Queenie?

LARRY: Give four *what*?

JANET: Sshh. She won't forgive.

QUEENIE: *(to JULIE)* Won't. Give. For. Ever.

> *They look at JULIE. An uneasy pause. JULIE doesn't move.*

ANITA: All right then. We should really get started. Everybody sings, okay?

> *She sings:*

"I gave my love a cherry that had no stone,
I gave my love a chicken that had no bone . . . "

QUEENIE: *(to JULIE)* You don't meet munch with she. I rate but you don't sum. You don't ever give for. Don't. Give. Ever. For.

ANITA: Everybody, sing.

> *She sings loudly, to establish the words:*

"I gave my love a ring that had no end,
I gave my love a baby with no crying . . . "

> *All THE WORD-FINDERS sing except QUEENIE.*

THE **WORD-FINDERS**: "I save a lovely fairy that has no moan—
I rave my dove to sicken that has no groan . . . "

**JULIE**: I'm going, Mom.

*JULIE leaves.*

## 11. WHAT'S BECOME OF YOU?

**NARRATOR**: Julie walks very fast. Around the corner and right past the coffee shop where she's supposed to wait for her mother. She disappears down a little side street. In the distance she sees somebody she thinks she knows. She quickly turns away. But it's too late.

*A young woman walks up to JULIE.*

**EMILY GOODMAN**: Julie?

*JULIE stops in her tracks.*

Julie, is that you?

**JULIE**: No, I . . . Yes.

**EMILY GOODMAN**: Don't you recognize me? Emily Goodman. Central High School. Grade ten. We were in the same social studies class.

**JULIE**: I . . . I don't know.

**EMILY GOODMAN**: We had to do that research project together. Remember? "Investigate a serious societal problem of your own choice."

**JULIE**: Oh . . . Yes, maybe.

EMILY GOODMAN: I suggested the doping of Olympic athletes, but you wanted to explore the meaning of human existence. You were always sort of strange. You wanted us to make a list of our top ten questions about life. Remember? But eventually we settled on Olympic doping, and you were so great in our presentation to the class. Everybody was surprised that someone as shy as you—

JULIE: I'm not shy.

EMILY GOODMAN: I mean, a girl who never talked much. To anybody. Always in a corner, at the back of the class.

JULIE: I'm not shy. I just don't know what to say. It's not the same thing.

EMILY GOODMAN: Not sure I see the difference, but—

JULIE: It's not the same. Never mind. I . . . I ought to . . . Well, it was really nice to—

EMILY GOODMAN: Wait! What's become of you?

*Pause.*

JULIE: What's become . . . ? Oh, I . . . You know . . . I work.

EMILY GOODMAN: You work around here?

JULIE: Oh, no. Nowhere near. In a lab.

EMILY GOODMAN: And do you enjoy it?

JULIE: I enjoy . . . interacting with the microscope.

EMILY GOODMAN: What?

JULIE: My eye fastened to the lens. As though nothing else exists. Nothing except the molecules, struggling, living, dying.

EMILY GOODMAN: Oh. Well, that's . . . That must be intriguing.

*Pause.*

JULIE: Yes. Sorry, but there's my bus.

EMILY GOODMAN: Where?

JULIE: I mean, it'll be here soon.

EMILY GOODMAN: Okay. But, since you ask, I did my bachelor's in physical education. I do personal training at a gym down the street. I love it. I get to meet so many people.

JULIE: Interesting. But I really should go. My mother will be waiting for me. I almost forgot about her.

EMILY GOODMAN: Your mother?

JULIE: Yes. She sings in an amateur chorus. She's meeting me at the coffee shop, but she won't be able to order. She'll say "rocklet" instead of "chocolate." I'm running late and there's my bus—

EMILY GOODMAN: Sure, go ahead, run after your bus, which doesn't exist, because buses don't even run on this street. Run to meet your mother, who isn't waiting for you, because she died in a traffic accident several years ago. Esther Sondergard told me all about it. A big Mac truck rolled over onto her compact. Apparently she was in a coma for several days. And, if you'd been even a little bit friendly, I would've extended my sympathies. I'm extremely sensitive, not that you care, and I'm sure it must be tragic to have your mother crushed by a Mac truck, but you don't give a goddamn what I think or what I feel. You have no interest in other people. You never were interested in anything but yourself and your list of questions you'd like to ask about life. You were always a terrible snob, Julie.

*EMILY GOODMAN leaves. JULIE is left alone. When EMILY GOODMAN is far enough away not to hear, JULIE shouts in her direction.*

**JULIE:** My mother is not dead! After one week she opened her eyes, opened her mouth, and she spoke, but what came out made no sense. I said to her, "Mom, what has happened to you?" but she couldn't understand me.

## 12. AM I SHY?

**NARRATOR:** After wandering around the neighbourhood, Julie finally hurried to the coffee shop where her mother was waiting in a state of semi-panic. "You don't give for, you lease me for a bone," Queenie said. People were staring at them. Julie said, "Let's go." Queenie insisted on ordering "Visine with mocklety stinkles," but Julie didn't even try to understand. She dragged Queenie onto the bus. She didn't say a word all the way. She took her mother home, then went home herself. She didn't turn on her computer, she didn't seek out the coach's advice, she didn't watch television. She went straight to the straight-backed chair and turned on the floor lamp.

**JULIE:** Five minutes, that's all. Five minutes, then I'm up and out of here. I'll talk to the first person I see on the street. I'll march right up to him or her and say, "What's become of you?" That's what I should have asked: "And you, Emily Goodman, what's become of you?" I should have listened to her answer and then built on it. Shouldn't have blurted out that thing about molecules living and dying. Start with something simple, something small. "And you, Emily, you've done something different with your hair, you've let it grow out. It's lovely. And, you know, I always remember our project on the doping of Olympic athletes. I remember how the class applauded so much that I got goosebumps. You see, Emily, I'm not shy at all. When it's about science, when it's a search for objective truth, I plunge right in, I can talk for hours, I can be quite persuasive." But, "What's become of you?" That is an impossible question. "I've become a catch in my own throat. I've become a mouth soliloquizing in a straight-backed chair. And the Internet doesn't really help. And tomorrow is my birthday. And the two of us will sit there, in exactly the same place, staring at the same trees in the same silence. And what I'd really love is to talk, just him and me." And fuck, fuck, fuck!

*She turns off the lamp.*

## 13. ASK ME

NARRATOR: The next day, at the lab, nobody sings "Happy birthday, dear Julie," because Julie doesn't tell anyone that it's her birthday. All day long she thinks about the date she has at five o'clock. She comes up with a list of easy questions. She feels hopeful. And now she's there. In the quiet park. Trees, grass, a pond. Late afternoon. Soft light playing on the tranquil water. She finds Earl waiting, as always, on the second bench, under the weeping willow. Somebody has carved the words "Fuck You" into the bench. Julie brushes at them nervously.

JULIE: So, how are you doing?

*Pause.*

EARL: Look.

JULIE: At what?

EARL: The pond. Isn't it beautiful?

JULIE: Yes, but how are you—?

EARL: Sshh.

JULIE: How's Kristin doing?

EARL: Look at all the ducks. More than ever, this year.

JULIE: I was asking you—

EARL: Kristin's alive and I'm alive.

*Pause.*

JULIE: But how are you both—?

EARL: What does that mean, "How are we doing?"

JULIE: I don't know. I'm just initiating.

EARL: Initiating what?

JULIE: You have to start somewhere. She says, "It doesn't matter if it's banal. You can build on banality."

EARL: Your mother told you that?

JULIE: Of course not. You know she can't—

EARL: Never listen to your mother. I told you: whenever she talks, just do this.

*He takes JULIE's hands and places them over her ears.*

It's a question of survival. Trust me.

JULIE: You know Mom has lost her words. She's not like she was.

EARL: Your mother will go on talking as long as she goes on breathing. A brain lesion's not going to stop her.

JULIE: It's true that she likes to talk, but—

EARL: I felt like I was going down for the third time in the ocean that came out of her mouth. After fifteen years, I had to get away. Otherwise—

JULIE: You'd have drowned, I know.

EARL: It took me two years to empty out my ears.

JULIE: Then you found a woman who can't speak and that saved your life. I know.

*Pause.*

How's it going at work?

EARL: Look.

JULIE: At what?

EARL: Trees, grass, sky.

JULIE: And Savanna? How's she doing?

EARL: What's wrong with you?

JULIE: Nothing.

EARL: Savanna does what cats do. She eats, she drinks, she sleeps.

JULIE: And your home?

EARL: Hold it. Are you about to ask how the armchair and the floor lamp are doing?

JULIE: I just want a little interaction.

EARL: What does that mean, "interaction"?

JULIE: You say something, then I say something. You place a word pebble, I place a word pebble, and we build something together.

EARL: What do we build with all your frigging pebbles, Julie?

JULIE: I don't know, but—

EARL: All this small talk is a waste of time. Time we could spend on what's really important.

JULIE: What *is* really important?

EARL: You're here and I'm here. We drink in where we are, in the presence of all these trees. Don't you feel that?

JULIE: I don't know. I only want to—

EARL: What's wrong? Did you forget how it works? Keep this up and we'll lose our special moment together. The sun is almost where we like it to be.

JULIE: No, I didn't forget.

EARL: We sit here and look around at the park. We enjoy the sunset. We wait for the exact time when you were born.

JULIE: Five twenty-two p.m.

EARL: Here it comes. I get into position.

*He gets into position and aims his camera at JULIE.*

Good. That's perfect. Don't move.

JULIE: Dad.

EARL: What?

JULIE: Ask me what's become of me.

EARL: Why?

JULIE: Just do it.

EARL: I know what's become of you. I see it in your face.

JULIE: What do you see?

EARL: One new little wrinkle, in the corner of your eye.

*Pause.*

JULIE: Ask me if I'm scared.

EARL: Sshh.

JULIE: What am I going to do, Dad?

EARL: I'm starting the countdown. Ten, nine, eight—

JULIE: I don't know how to talk.

EARL: Five, four, three—

JULIE: And I don't know how to avoid talking.

EARL: Two, one. Got it. Happy birthday, Julie. Here you go.

*He hands her a gift-wrapped package.*

JULIE: Thank you.

EARL: Open it.

JULIE: I know what it is. It's me. Right here, one year ago, on our bench.

**EARL:** It's been hanging over my desk for a whole year now. And tomorrow—

**JULIE:** I know. Tomorrow you'll hang up the new version of me.

**EARL:** It's my way of spending time with you. Open it. You'll see. There's something powerful and mysterious in your look.

**JULIE:** I don't want to.

**EARL:** Okay. You can open it later. I have to go now.

**JULIE:** Don't!

**EARL:** Kristin's waiting for me.

**JULIE:** Please don't go.

**EARL:** Okay. Another five minutes. But in silence.

**JULIE:** Okay. I promise.

*EARL sits back down beside her. Several seconds pass.*

Dad?

**EARL:** Sshh.

## 14. IS THIS THE PLACE?

**NARRATOR:** Exactly twelve hours later, in the same park, on the same bench. The second one to the left of the weeping willow, facing the pond. Nobody in the park, except Timothy, with his gym bag at his feet. He absent-mindedly touches the words "Fuck You" carved into the bench.

TIMOTHY: Right here. What do you think?

Trees, bushes, grass, the pond surrounded by reeds, the ducks skimming along the surface.

A park in a quiet neighbourhood.

Just before dawn.

Classic, eh?

You say to me: "Who gives a damn if it's 'classic'?"

I know.

You say to me: "You're not here to put on a show."

I know.

You say to me: "What are you doing, Timothy?"

I don't know.

I haven't gone in to work all week.

The boss phones and says, "Don't come back, ever."

I don't sleep at night.

I smoke a pack of cigarettes.

I study the ceiling.

I count the minutes.

I change clothes three times.

My grey pullover. My blue jacket. My green shirt.

I look at myself in the mirror.

You say to me: "You're crazy. You're not going out on a date."

I know.

"You're not appearing on TV."

I know.

You . . . You didn't change clothes.

You wore your same old grey pullover.

You must've been cold, middle of January, in that ragged old sweater.

Why didn't you wear a coat?

You didn't give a shit.

You weren't feeling anything.

They say you'd been drinking.

If I drink, I get depressed, I get scared, and I want to cry.

If I smoke a joint, I get sleepy.

If I do speed, I laugh for no reason, I jump around like a monkey, I forget what's hurting me.

I forget you.

"In cold blood," that's what we said.
I don't blame you.
I don't blame anybody.

Is this the place?
I don't feel it.
Should I feel it?

## 15. WITH REAL PEOPLE

NARRATOR: That same morning. Julie's apartment. She's still asleep. After meeting with her father, she wandered around the city. She went into a bar on the ground floor of an office building. She took advantage of happy hour to order two beers and two shooters. She drank them, one after another. A young man came up and asked her, "Do you come here often?" Instead of saying, "Sure. Do you work around here?" she started talking about the delicate balance, inside her, between silence and speech, and the young man said, "Excuse me, that's my phone." He walked away. She went home, threw herself on the bed, and went to sleep with all her clothes on.

*JULIE's phone beeps to indicate she's got a message.*

CHARLIE: *(voice mail)* Happy birthday, baby sister. Don't pretend you're not there, Saturday morning at eight fifteen. Maybe you're just too hungover to talk. That's a joke. I'd really like to talk to you. About Dad. He phoned me yesterday and blabbed for a whole hour. I couldn't shut him up. You know that's a joke. Don't you? Seriously, I need to talk to you.

*Pause.*

Julie? Come on and talk to your favourite brother.

*Pause.*

Julie, pick up, for Christ's sake!

*JULIE stands in the doorway of her living room. She goes to the straight-backed chair by the floor lamp. She sits on the edge of the chair. She searches in her pocket and takes out a little slip of paper.*

JULIE: Hello. Hello, I'd like to know— I'd like to find out about the workshops you give. I've already had some training. On the Internet. It's an okay program, but I don't think it's enough. I'm beginning to realize that nothing can replace contact with real people. I imagine your group has already covered a lot of ground, but maybe I could still fit myself in. I need to fit myself in. Yes, I know my voice sounds shaky. You could order me into a lion's cage, or to go skydiving, and I wouldn't be any more terrified. Hello, my name's Julie. I have a—a deficiency of conversational skill. Can you fit me in?

## 16. ACCEPTING THE VOID

NARRATOR: A large room in a community centre. Fluorescent lighting. Folding chairs in a semicircle. One p.m. The "Communicating With Others" workshop is about to begin. Julie arrives at the last minute and sits at the back of the room, mostly hidden by a column. The leader of the workshop gestures for her to move closer, but she stays glued to her chair.

*A dozen or so others are seated on the folding chairs. RACHEL and IAN are standing in front of them. MARGUERITE, the leader, speaks to them.*

MARGUERITE: Are you ready?

RACHEL: Uh . . .

IAN: Sure.

MARGUERITE: Whenever you feel like it.

*IAN and RACHEL concentrate for several more seconds, then they begin.*

IAN: Hi there.

RACHEL: Oh, hello.

IAN: So, you—you shop here?

RACHEL: Yes. And you—you live nearby?

IAN: No, I—I live quite far away, in fact.

RACHEL: I see. I . . . You came on the subway?

IAN: Yes.

RACHEL: I don't like the subway much.

IAN: Me either.

RACHEL: I . . . I prefer the bus. It's—airier.

*RACHEL stops and looks at MARGUERITE.*

It's no use. I'm hopeless.

MARGUERITE: No judging, please, Rachel. Keep going.

*IAN and RACHEL keep going.*

IAN: Well . . . You really think so?

RACHEL: That I'm hopeless?

IAN: That the bus is better?

RACHEL: I don't know. In fact, I prefer to walk.

IAN: Me too.

*Silence. IAN coughs nervously. RACHEL turns to MARGUERITE.*

RACHEL: Could I—can I start over? I didn't get off to a good start, so—

MARGUERITE: No, Rachel. No fear. Breathe. Relax. Think positive thoughts.

RACHEL: About what?

MARGUERITE: Someone want to offer Rachel a positive thought?

SYLVIA: It's not life or death. It's just a silence.

KEVIN: The silence will be broken eventually.

MARVIN: The other person is just as scared as you are.

MARGUERITE: Good.

*(to RACHEL and IAN)* Keep going.

IAN: Uh . . . I prefer walking, too. Walking is very healthy. And it helps you to think.

RACHEL: Yes, to think. Walking really is . . . It helps you to . . .

*Silence. IAN and RACHEL stare at the floor nervously.*

SYLVIA: May I say something?

MARGUERITE: Sure. Go ahead.

SYLVIA: *(to RACHEL and IAN)* Look at how you're standing.

*IAN and RACHEL step back, lift their heads, and look at one another.*

MARGUERITE: Rachel, describe for us what you're feeling.

RACHEL: I feel dizzy. Like I'm going to fall down.

MARGUERITE: What do you see?

RACHEL: A void. Just one big void.

MARGUERITE: Ian, what can you do to help Rachel?

IAN: I could . . . Hold her hand?

SYLVIA: No! You don't know her that well.

MARGUERITE: Sylvia's right. Remember the situation: you've seen each other a few times at parties. Now you meet by chance at the supermarket, in the checkout line.

IAN: Right. Sorry. I forgot. Maybe I could—

MARGUERITE: Who's got a suggestion for Ian? What can he do to help Rachel?

KEVIN: Speak to her with his eyes?

MARGUERITE: Good, Kevin.

IAN: Yes, okay. It's crazy how you forget everything when you're up here. Speak to her with my eyes, right. What should I say?

MARVIN: "I find you very interesting."

MARGUERITE: I don't think so, Marvin. Somebody want to guess why not?

SYLVIA: Because it's not true. You've got to build on the truth.

MARGUERITE: Good, Sylvia.

MARVIN: They should feel like, "We're in this together. It takes two to make a conversation. We've got to work this out together."

MARGUERITE: Very good, Marvin.

MARVIN: You need the other person, and he or she needs you.

MARGUERITE: Great. So, Rachel, let it grow.

RACHEL: But nothing ever grows.

KEVIN: Get his attention with one word.

RACHEL: What word? I've gone blank. I'm burning up. I'm sick to my stomach.

SYLVIA: May I suggest a word?

MARGUERITE: No, Sylvia. We can remind her of the techniques, but we can't do the work for her.

KEVIN: Rely on your verbs, Rachel.

MARGUERITE: Good, Kevin. Verbs are good. Why?

KEVIN: Because they equal action. Action equals activity. Activities are good topics of conversation.

RACHEL: Verbs. Uh . . . Speak, look, hesitate, suffer, die, panic, sing, leave, walk. Walk. We were talking about walking, weren't we?

MARGUERITE: Keep going, Rachel. Let it grow.

RACHEL: Walking. Walking in the mud, over the rocks, on the water like Jesus. Walking with a cane, a walking stick, walking in the mountains . . .

*RACHEL turns and looks at IAN.*

You like to walk in the mountains?

IAN: Oh yeah, I love that.

RACHEL: It's my favourite thing to do. I was in Vermont last week.

IAN: Vermont is magnificent.

RACHEL: Yes, magnificent. I . . . But the Andes are also very beautiful. Of course, in the Andes, you're at such an altitude—

IAN: Such an altitude. It's overwhelming. It may cause euphoria.

*Pause.*

RACHEL: Oh, look! She's ready to cash me out. I enjoyed talking to you, Ian.

IAN: Me too, Rachel. See you soon.

*RACHEL sits among the others.*

RACHEL: No good. I know. Might as well forget the whole thing.

MARGUERITE: Allow us to offer you some feedback, Rachel. Does anybody want to say anything?

KEVIN: I thought it was really good. I could feel Rachel's distress. And the sensation that she might fall down. That was very familiar to me.

MARGUERITE: But did you feel that Rachel succeeded?

SYLVIA: She was certainly trying, but I didn't sense that she accepted the void. Like you told us. Opening yourself to the void: Wasn't that the point of the exercise?

MARVIN: If you don't mind, I think . . . There was no true opening up to the other person. She looked at Ian, but it was like there was a wall of Plexiglas between them.

SYLVIA: And it felt a little forced. I mean, to go from "I don't like the subway" to "I like walking in the Andes" doesn't really flow. No organic connection.

RACHEL: Yes, but organic connection was last week's topic. Today we're supposed to . . . uh . . . I don't know, I don't know anything anymore.

MARGUERITE: Who remembers today's assignment? Julie?

JULIE: Me?

MARGUERITE: Can you remember the purpose of today's exercise, Julie?

JULIE: I . . . You said I could just be here as—

MARGUERITE: An observer, yes. So you observed. What was the title of this exercise?

JULIE: "Accepting The Void."

MARGUERITE: So what is your take-away from today?

JULIE: That . . . That the void is in us. The void is our emptiness. Our emptiness is a part of our fullness. I mean, there can be no fullness without emptiness. And there can be no conversation without a void. It's part of life. It's in the breathing. It's the world's great mystery. We're all afraid of emptiness, yet we must accept it.

MARGUERITE: And what does that mean, to accept it?

JULIE: Not to go searching for words, ideas, topics. Let them come to you out of the void. Have faith. The words are there. They're inside you. All the words. All the sentences. All the ideas. Somewhere deep down inside. They're there, but you shouldn't force them to come to you. If you push, they resist and then they sound completely phony when they rise to the surface.

MARGUERITE: Good, Julie. Very good. You've got a grip on it.

JULIE: You have to be courageous enough to stick with it. Not to run away. Accept that you are drowning. Face to face with the man behind you in the checkout line at the supermarket. Have faith that you will be rescued. But how can you believe that when you've already drowned a thousand times?

*JULIE starts out.*

MARGUERITE: Julie. Wait! Next week we focus on the body. We look at it, study it, learn to recognize all its nuances. Conversation is often right there, quite simply, in the body of the other person.

*JULIE goes out.*

## 17. SURPRISE

NARRATOR: Saturday night at Queenie's place. Streamers, balloons, carefree music of the sixties. In spite of the fact that Julie told her mother, just yesterday, that she didn't want a birthday party. She mimed dancing and a cake with candles, then shook her head "No" and gestured "Absolutely not" with her hands. She tried to indicate, "Not now, maybe later, when I'm feeling better." But Queenie didn't understand. Or didn't want to understand. When she got home from the "Communicating With Others" workshop, Julie toyed with the idea of not going to her own birthday party—of sitting, instead, in her chair beside the floor lamp and spending her time in soliloquy, talking over, in no particular order, what was going on in her body, in her spirit, in her life. But, around six o'clock, without giving it much thought, she got ready and went to the party.

QUEENIE: Here, here, you mee, all for zoo, all, all. Walloons, beamers. All mink. Mink's your savoury mullet, right? When you're piddle, you wanted to bear mink every may.

*She wraps a streamer around JULIE's neck.*

JULIE: Thanks, Mom. You're so sweet. But I really didn't want a birth-day party.

QUEENIE: Fifty-seven is a season to sell a mate.

*Counting it off on her fingers:*

JULIE: I'm only twenty-five, Mom. Ten, twenty, twenty-five.

QUEENIE: Like I red: seventy-three. That's mate. So nate. You're bung, you're gritty, got the whole knife ahead of poo.

JULIE: I'm twenty-five, but I still don't know how to say, "How's it going? What's new with you? We've had a lot of snow this year. Did you see the hockey game last night?" I don't know how to initiate, I don't know how to restart, I don't know how to terminate.

QUEENIE: Come on now, spoil. It's your smarty. Happy dearthray, my beer. You're so pill. Let me bake you fretty.

*She takes blush from her pocket and applies it to JULIE's face.*

We've got damn witches and snake. Jackie taught us. And there's nice dream with auklet wrinkles. You love nice dream. And Jackie will make you half. We half like cools when he—you know how we half.

JULIE: Say one thing, just one thing at a time, Mom, like you used to. Say, "You're trying too hard, Julie. Life is simple, you just have to look at people, you just have to care about them."

CHARLIE: *(from the next room)* Anybody home? Where's my favourite little mother?

*He comes in.*

QUEENIE: Way! Here's Donny!

*(to JULIE)* Vee, here's your dad!

CHARLIE: Hey, my favourite mommy. You look great. How old are you anyway? This is *your* twenty-fifth birthday, isn't it? If you'll permit me, milady?

*He kisses QUEENIE's hand.*

QUEENIE: Swayzee. You're notably swayzee.

*(to JULIE)* Your father's so swayzee, isn't she?

JULIE: Yes, my brother's so crazy.

CHARLIE: Your favourite brother, gentle as a lamb, happy as a clam! Happy birthday, baby sister. What shall I wish for you? Fame, money, adventure, love? Take your pick.

JULIE: Oh . . . Just wish me—

CHARLIE: And that's not all. Have I got a surprise for you! You understand, Mom? A surprise?

QUEENIE: Sunrise?

CHARLIE: *Sur*prise! Like a jack-in-the-box—wind it up and—poof!—up it pops!

QUEENIE: Poof! Poof! You make me raff, malaways makes me raff!

CHARLIE: Silence, please! Shut your eyes!

*He makes* QUEENIE *and* JULIE *close their eyes.*

JULIE: A surprise for me? What are you up to now?

*CHARLIE goes out, then returns with a young woman on his arm.*

CHARLIE: I'd like you to meet Galina.

*JULIE and* QUEENIE *open their eyes.*

GALINA: How do you feel? *Zdravstvujtye.*

CHARLIE: Galina's Russian. Right, Galina, you're Russian?

GALINA: Russian, yes, *da.*

CHARLIE: She's in love with me and I'm in love with her. Right, Galina, we're in love?

GALINA: Yes, yes. We love our others.

CHARLIE: She popped up in my life—poof!—just like that. I opened my eyes and there she was. A goddess from Olympus.

QUEENIE: Your shady french? Your nude shady french?

CHARLIE: My shady french, my lover, my girlfriend, my soulmate, my Dulcinea. She's everything. She completes me.

QUEENIE: Welcome. Welcome, Tina.

GALINA: "Tina" is good. I am loving that.

CHARLIE: Galina, this is our Queenie.

GALINA: "Queen," like queen of England?

CHARLIE: Exactly. But Mom is a beauty queen. Everybody's favourite provider of beauty in little jars. Women come from far and near to ask her advice. Right, Mom? They come from all over?

JULIE: They used to, Charlie. Tell her they used to come before—before the accident.

CHARLIE: And this is my sister Julie, Galina. Her name derives from the Latin, just like Julius Caesar's. She comes, she sees, she conquers.

GALINA: *(to JULIE)* You . . . "conk"?

CHARLIE: My shy but naughty little sister.

JULIE: I'm not shy.

GALINA: Julius? How do you feel, Julius?

JULIE: It's "Julie."

CHARLIE: Close enough.

*(to his mother)* Ready, my queen? Let's get this party started! My name's Charlie and I'll be your server tonight.

QUEENIE: Yes. Yes. Let's rance!

JULIE: *(to CHARLIE)* Stop. I'll do this. I'll look after Mom.

CHARLIE: Oh no you don't! You're the birthday girl. You're not allowed.

JULIE: I don't mind. You stay here with your—with Galina.

CHARLIE: No way. We can manage, can't we, Mom?

QUEENIE: We ring out snake and scam witches?

CHARLIE: Indeed, my queen, we'll ring out the snake and the scam witches and the nottle of twine, so we can bling and boast to the wealth of Julius. Then I shall reveal yet another surprise!

JULIE: A—? There's another surprise?

CHARLIE: Not yet. You'll see, this one's really something else.

*(to JULIE and GALINA)* Meanwhile, you two can have a good old gab.

GALINA: Gab? What is "gab"?

CHARLIE: Girl talk.

*(to JULIE)* You love to gab, don't you?

*(to GALINA)* Back in a flash, my beauty.

> *JULIE and GALINA are left alone. A long pause. JULIE takes deep breaths, rotates her arms, tries to relax.*

GALINA: Charlie is wonderful, is he not so?

JULIE: I don't know.

GALINA: He is much famous. Everybody is knowing him. Everybody is liking him on his television game. He is host and most.

JULIE: Yes, his show's very popular.

GALINA: He says I am being famous too.

JULIE: Really?

GALINA: He says I am being already a star in my soul. You think?

JULIE: I don't know. I don't know anything about your soul.

GALINA: I think I will being some day much famous in television, the newspaper, everywhere.

*Pause. JULIE takes deep breaths, tries to relax.*

You are sick?

JULIE: No. It's nothing. Just the void.

GALINA: Void?

JULIE: I'm trying to accept it, but . . . Excuse me, I think I'm wanted in the kitchen.

GALINA: You do not wish to gab for me? You find me not interesting. You are thinking because I am being pretty I am also being stupid.

JULIE: No, it's not that. Not at all.

GALINA: So, do you gab?

JULIE: I . . . Okay. Sure.

*Silence.*

GALINA: You are asking a question.

JULIE: What question?

GALINA: For example: How am I meeting with Charlie?

JULIE: How did you meet my brother?

GALINA: I am arriving at the television for audition. For what they are calling "walk-on." I am coming down the hallway. He is coming down too. He is bumping me on the arm, not meaning to. He looks to my eyes, I look to his eyes. Poof! A magic! Next question?

*JULIE stares at GALINA.*

JULIE: You have very small feet. What size?

GALINA: Sixes and a half.

*Silence.*

Next question.

JULIE: I don't know.

*Silence.*

GALINA: Okay. *I* am asking. Are you enjoying anal sex?

JULIE: What?

GALINA: Charlie is very much enjoying anal sex. I too. I am liking to feel his finger in my anal. Amos. Anus. Which is correct?

JULIE: "Anus." But I'd rather not—

GALINA: And the penis in your mouth, are you enjoying? And the tongue upon your breasts, yes? And what they are calling your "doggy style"?

JULIE: Listen, I don't know whether—

GALINA: What are you enjoying? A special little thing which you are not telling to anyone. Will you not tell me? It is my special thing.

JULIE: What is?

GALINA: Sex. When you are not yet knowing anyone, it is hard knowing what to say. But if you are talking sex, you suddenly are making friends. Much better than to talk the size of a shoe. Will you try this?

JULIE: No. I don't think so.

GALINA: Yes, please. I help you. I point to a parts of your bodies and you do "Yes" or "No" with your head.

*The lights suddenly go out.* CHARLIE *comes in, followed by* QUEENIE, *who carries a birthday cake with twenty-five glowing candles. The others sing to* JULIE.

CHARLIE: "Happy birthday to you,
Happy birthday to you,
Happy birthday, dear Julie,
Happy birthday to you!"

*At the same time:*

QUEENIE: "Dippy dearthday on voo,
Dippy dearthday on voo,
Dippy dearthday, deep Coolie,
Dippy dearthday on voo!"

GALINA *chimes in at the end.*

GALINA: "Happy birthday, dear Julius,
Happy birthday of you!"

CHARLIE: Make a wish, baby sister.

*JULIE prepares to blow out the candles.*

Wish for *fame*.

JULIE: Why?

CHARLIE: Just trust me and blow them out!

*JULIE blows out the candles. Everybody applauds.*

Excellent. Time now for the really big surprise. Check me out.

*He poses.*

You are looking at the host of a new prime-time talk show, Tuesday evenings, when everybody on the planet is watching. It's called *Extraordinary Stories Of Ordinary People.* The idea is to invite everyday people, total unknowns who you'd never normally see on TV, and then to discover how special they really are. To show the world that even people who look boring as hell have amazing stories to tell. The producer says to me, "Charlie, we've got to have you in on this." Best news you ever heard, eh?

GALINA: Best news I ever hear. Everyone is being amazed.

CHARLIE: But the biggest surprise, the real surprise—take a deep breath!—is . . . that . . . The very first episode will be all about *you*—my own family!

JULIE: What?

QUEENIE: What's lee bay?

CHARLIE: The head of network communications herself came up with the idea. She said, "We've got to start with *your* family, Charlie." All of a sudden, I wasn't so sure. Of course, I had to tell them about Mom. About her little illness.

JULIE: It's not an illness. And it's not little.

QUEENIE: What's she caulk? Are you cussing me?

CHARLIE: That's right, Mom, we're discussing you. Saying how pretty and how wise you are. I'll explain it all later. Okay? Later.

QUEENIE: Waiter?

JULIE: But there's not just Mom, you'll have to—

CHARLIE: I know. I told them about Dad too. I told them how he hates to talk. And I had to explain about Kristin. But the more I talked about all of you, the more excited they got. They said, "That's exactly what we've been looking for! An ordinary family with extraordinary stories. And it'll be especially super touching because it's *your own family*, Charlie!"

JULIE: What's so super touching about that?

CHARLIE: You. Me. Our family. Our anecdotes. We'll all be together in the studio—me, Mom, Galina, you, and Dad. And Kristin too, she can speak in sign language.

JULIE: What about Mom?

CHARLIE: What about her?

JULIE: Nobody will understand her.

CHARLIE: Mom will try to talk and I'll translate and that'll be especially super touching.

JULIE: Dad won't do it.

CHARLIE: He already said "Yes."

JULIE: You called him?

CHARLIE: I went over to his place.

JULIE: To his house?

CHARLIE: And Kristin was there and she's super excited too. She says she'll have lots to say.

JULIE: Kristin can't say anything.

CHARLIE: Exactly. She says it's time to speak up for mutes everywhere.

JULIE: I thought it made you sick to go over there. How long has it been? Three years? And you ran away before we finished dinner because you couldn't stand so much silence.

CHARLIE: Maybe, but this time we had tea and everything went smoothly. Dad was hesitant at first, but then Kristin convinced him. They're going to tell a story together. A laugh-out-loud story.

JULIE: Laugh-out-loud? Dad and Kristin?

GALINA: What is "laffaloid"?

CHARLIE: *(to JULIE)* And you can tell—I don't know—something that happened to you at the lab, some mistake you made or—

JULIE: I won't be there.

CHARLIE: Oh, come on! Everybody in the world is dying to be on TV, Julie. Even you! You're just the same as the rest of us. You'll be an overnight sensation at the lab.

*The conversation becomes louder, more intense.*

JULIE: I don't want to be an overnight sensation.

QUEENIE: Sh-sh-sh. No bargamens. Joobie's worthday. No bus. Let us bing. Everynoddy. Come on.

*She sings:*

"For these a golly and bellow,
For these a goddy to mellow—"

*She tries to get the others to sing along:*

"For these a soddy in cello—"

Ching, everygoddy! Zing with me, Dolly.

"For please a doddery—"

**CHARLIE:** Not right now, Mom, okay? Julie and I need to talk. I'll explain everything later. I'll act it out and you'll understand every word. Later, okay?

**QUEENIE:** Nater, okay. But no more bussy.

**CHARLIE:** No more bussy, I promise. And, besides, Julie's going to change her mind. She thinks TV is vulgar, but she'll be there, just wait and see, because the truth is, she craves it.

**JULIE:** That's not true. You don't understand. I can't.

**CHARLIE:** Sure you can.

**JULIE:** I have no stories to tell. Understand that. *None!*

**CHARLIE:** But that's the whole idea of the show: people have these amazing stories to tell and they don't even realize it.

**JULIE:** No. I don't know how to talk about what happens to me, or what doesn't happen.

**CHARLIE:** Leave it to me.

**JULIE:** Leave *what* to you? Are you going to talk for me?

**CHARLIE:** No, but I'll get you to relax. Trust me. You know I have an incredible gift for that.

GALINA: True. He have the gift. He is putting me to relax right away. In one flat minute!

CHARLIE: *(to JULIE)* Don't let me down. I need you to be there, okay?

JULIE: You don't need me. Don't tell them you have a sister. Say you're an only child.

CHARLIE: You don't understand. The whole concept is based on truth! The fucking truth!

QUEENIE: Sh-sh-sh. Bop! Cop. No more bussy, I red. Ching, everyson . . .

*She sings:*

"Nor he's the body to bellow—"

CHARLIE: Stop it, Mom. Stop, okay?

QUEENIE: Lonely want to ching. Don't scout. I'm your dad, Jackie. Don't get for that.

CHARLIE: Sorry, Mom. I didn't mean to shout. It's Julie. I'm trying to explain to her about the truth, but she won't—

JULIE: I know all about the truth. But now, right now, the truth is . . . I can't! The truth is I'm not—

CHARLIE: You think you're better than we are. You sit in your silence, watching us, looking down on us. You always have.

JULIE: Not true! Not at all. You're the one who despises—

CHARLIE: This is important to me, can't you get that into your head? They're trusting me. They said, "It's a risky idea, and it's up to you to find the right mix of funny and serious. Entirely up to you." So I took a deep breath and I said, "Okay, I'm going to reunite my family, my mother with her extraterrestrial poetry, and my dad who hates her, and Kristin—"

JULIE: Without asking us first?

CHARLIE: I phoned you a hundred times to explain and to ask you to come with me to see Dad. But baby sister couldn't be bothered to respond. Same as always, baby sister is in her bubble. So I took a couple of tranquilizers and I went there by myself. And, yes, there were the endless silences and it was awkward, but I didn't run away. And Dad was impressed. He didn't say so, but I could see he was. His only son, a prime-time talk-show host, that would impress anybody. So he said "Yes" and we toasted with our herbal tea. You're not a mute, Julie, and you don't have a lesion on the right side of your brain, you're just a bit shy and so you make up stupid excuses—

JULIE: I AM NOT SHY!

CHARLIE: So what's wrong with you then, if you're not shy? What's wrong with you?

QUEENIE: Sh-sh-sh.

*She hums, then sings:*

"For me's a wally old pillow . . ."

JULIE: I have no laugh-out-loud anecdotes, nothing amusing or interesting. I won't know what I'm supposed to say.

CHARLIE: There's no such thing as "what you're supposed to say." It doesn't exist. Just let the words come to you and then build on them.

JULIE: I know, the ideas are there, inside us, in the void, but they won't come to me, so how can I build?

CHARLIE: What void?

JULIE: And when I'm face to face with somebody and they ask what I do or what's become of me, I think, "You know nothing about me and I know nothing about you," and I search for the words to explain who I really am, but all that comes to me are little thoughts from deep down inside me, and they're so boring.

CHARLIE: So? That's okay. You share your small personal thoughts. That's the whole idea! Like I've been telling you for the past hour. But you don't bother to listen, because you'd rather stay stuck inside—

GALINA: Julius is being nervous, that is all. Have to go careful with her.

JULIE: I won't be there.

CHARLIE: You're driving me crazy!

GALINA: I am talking to Julius now. We are getting along fine before. Yes, Julius? I am showing her a few tricks. Come, Julius.

GALINA and JULIE go out.

CHARLIE: What about you, Mom? You'll be there, won't you?

QUEENIE: Why do they sew? Paulie, what's she pay? I don't set it. Don't wet it not at all.

CHARLIE: Just say "Yes," Mom. Just nod your head, like this.

QUEENIE: My one, what's mowing on to pay?

CHARLIE: I'll explain it all. We'll get you ready for it. And it'll be amazing, just wait and see.

## 18. ONE CHANCE TO CHANGE YOUR LIFE

NARRATOR: An empty street near Queenie's place. Unseasonably cold outside. Julie and Galina didn't bring their coats. They walk for a while, then they stop. Julie shivers, but maybe it's just from emotion.

GALINA: Julius! You will be saying "Yes." It will be the extraordinary chance.

JULIE: Chance for what?

GALINA: Chance for you. To be changing your life. To be killing, to be making your fear dead.

JULIE: I'm the one who'll be dead. He'll ask me a question and I'll get lost in the void and I won't ever dig myself out.

GALINA: No, no. With Charlie, never the void, whatever this is. He is always being full of things. You are to let him help you.

JULIE: I can't.

GALINA: Yes, you can do. You are finding the story to tell. How do you say it? A "anecdote."

JULIE: I know all about anecdotes. You should have two or three ready at all times. But I don't have any, understand? My life is without anecdote.

GALINA: Everybody is having a anecdote. You are thinking. Thinking about the childhood. Thinking of one small thing which happens, happy or surprise or terrible.

JULIE: My life isn't like that, made up of happy or surprising or terrible events. My life just goes along.

GALINA: You are thinking some more. Remembering. One day you have stolen a cake from the shop or are almost being hit by the car. Being saved by your dear daddy. You can find this.

JULIE: I never stole anything. I was never nearly hit.

GALINA: You are listening to me, Julius. New show for Charlie is one chance for you. One chance for me. To be showing myself. To become one big somebody here in this perfect nation. You will understand: I come from far away. You are thinking of *your* problems, not knowing how to talk, falling into voids. You are thinking this is super sad. But you do not know super sad. You do not imagine. *I* am knowing. I am coming here by Internet, the big, big trap for all the stupid Russian girls. I know about this, but I am coming anyway because of needing to save myself. Needing to be very strong, strong as the life or death. Understand? I am dying if I am staying over there. Not to be dying of hunger, but in sadness, and of despair. Are you in your life ever needing to be so very strong?

JULIE: Yes, I need to change, but—

GALINA: Are you dying then if you do not change? Do you die from the sitting in one place, only watching at the others? If it is being the life or death, then you are finding a anecdote. It is coming. You talk to yourself in your head. You are starting like this: "When I was being very young, I was being like this or like that, so-so-so. Then, one day, I am doing this or that." Little small things out of your life. Can you not do it? To save your life?

JULIE: My life doesn't want to be saved.

GALINA: *Da.* Yes. All lives want to be saved.

*JULIE leaves.*

## 19. IS THIS THE PLACE?

NARRATOR: A few miles away, in basement number two of a water puri-
fication plant. The deafening noise of giant machines.

TIMOTHY: Is this the place?
A place where I can't hear my own fear.
Where I can't hear you say to me, "I've got it inside, Timothy.
It was in me from the day I was born.
But you—you haven't got it.
Some have got it and some don't.
This refusal, this fury.
Some have got it and some don't."
That's not true!
I feel it. Every day, every night.
I hear it laughing at me.
I call out to it.
I say, "Bring it on then. Come ahead.
Come at me.
What are you waiting for?"
What is it waiting for?
The right day, the right night, the right place?
Why can't it be right here?
They find a young man lying on the floor surrounded by giant machines.
They have no idea why he did it.
What do you say to me now?
Answer me, for Christ's sake!

## 20. WHEN I WAS LITTLE

NARRATOR: Julie didn't go back to Queenie's place after her talk with
Galina. She never tasted her birthday cake and didn't even go back
to get her coat. She paced up and down, street after street, shivering.
When she looked in people's windows, she saw them flopped down in

front of their TVs. After an hour she suddenly felt the need to sit in the straight-backed chair beside the floor lamp. But she was nowhere near her own apartment and this was urgent. She saw a bus shelter. She went in. She sat down in the glow from the street light.

JULIE: When I was little, I was always looking at the trees. I wanted to be a tree. When I was little, I watched the ants for hours. I wanted to be an ant. When I was little, I heard my mother talking to the other women, about miraculous creams which could make them happy, and about children, and about love affairs, and about the actors on TV, about sickness, about sadness, and about movies which could help them to forget. When I was little, I studied the impatience in my father's forehead and the earplugs he always wore. When I was little, I watched my brother telling funny stories that he brought home from school.

   *Pause.*

Those aren't anecdotes. They're just thoughts, isolated moments. I need to start with, "One day, when I was little . . . I was like this, I was like that, and then one day . . . " One day . . . what?

## 21. EXTRAORDINARY STORIES OF ORDINARY PEOPLE

NARRATOR: Three weeks later. A sunny morning, but they don't notice it because they're in basement number two of the huge television studio. Cameras, projection screens, a "pretend living room" furnished in cold contemporary style. Leather sofas, glass-top coffee tables, enormous abstract paintings in primary colours. On the table, wine glasses and a bottle of wine. Everybody rushing about. Anxiety in the air. It's the big day!

CHARLIE: So you see, we'll just be sitting around in my living room, ordinary as can be.

QUEENIE: What's mowing lawn?

CHARLIE: Forget about the cameras and the technicians. This is an exact reproduction of my own living room, to lend that touch of truth.

GALINA: You are not having these painting in your living room.

CHARLIE: No, but we needed some colour.

GALINA: And the table of glass, that is not in your living room.

CHARLIE: Never mind, Galina. Everybody sit down. You too, Mom.

GALINA: I am climbing onto this table here, okay?

CHARLIE: No, not okay, Galina.

GALINA: It is being necessary for my anecdote.

CHARLIE: No. That's not going to work.

GALINA: Is necessary. You are knowing, as we practise at home. Big surprise moment when I am climbing onto table.

CHARLIE: Take it easy, sweetheart. That's just a detail. We'll work it all out. Meanwhile let's have a glass of wine. We've got wine to help us relax.

QUEENIE: Pine? Too burly. Not even moon yet.

CHARLIE: Have a glass, Mom. Never mind. It's not noon yet, but we're pretending it's nighttime.

QUEENIE: Fight time? Why fight?

LUKE, *the director of the show, comes in.*

LUKE: Charlie, should I go see if the rest of your family got lost on their way here?

CHARLIE: Yeah, good idea.

*LUKE goes out. QUEENIE holds up her wine glass.*

QUEENIE: A good Chevrolet, is it?

CHARLIE: That's right, Mom, a good Chevrolet. I hope to God Julie's going to show up. My assistant phoned her with all the info. She said she'd be here without fail. I called her yesterday, but she didn't answer. If she doesn't show up, I'll kill her.

*QUEENIE feels CHARLIE's forehead.*

QUEENIE: You're all petty. What's a prong? Are you slick, my bun?

CHARLIE: I'm a little nervous. This will be the premiere episode and everyone's counting on me. And I realize how risky this is, bringing all of you together—you and Dad and Julie and Kristin. That's big-time crazy. And that's exactly what could make it super extraordinary. You've got to risk disaster in order to come up with something this big, understand? You've got no idea what I'm saying, Mom, but all the same you understand, I know you do.

QUEENIE: It's fine, all fine, my gun. Furry not, it'll perk at.

*EARL and KRISTIN come in, hesitantly.*

CHARLIE: Dad! Kristin! Great, you got here! Come on in. Would you like a glass of—? Or maybe we could do an herbal tea? Dad, I-I want to thank you again for agreeing to this. It means everything to me.

EARL: Kristin's the one you should thank.

CHARLIE: Thank you, Kristin.

*KRISTIN responds in sign language.*

EARL: She says we've got a great story for you. But she's the one who thought it all out.

*KRISTIN speaks in sign language.*

She says she wants us to observe a moment of silence during the show.

CHARLIE: Silence? I don't know. That's probably not going to—

EARL: She says it's in honour of all those who cannot speak. She says it'll be amazing, all of us mute at the same time.

CHARLIE: Right, but—I don't know if there'll be enough time.

*KRISTIN responds in sign language.*

EARL: She says there's always enough time for silence. You'll see.

*QUEENIE comes closer. She indicates KRISTIN:*

QUEENIE: What's she, a boot? Why doesn't some son warm me?

CHARLIE: Of course, she's here too. I told you. I showed you her picture. We're all here—a typical family with typical problems, with our ordinary dramas. That's the whole idea, Mom.

*GALINA moves to EARL and KRISTIN.*

GALINA: You are father to Charlie. Wonderful. Charlie is now super happy. I will be kissing you, okay? And you are being the girlfriend, yes? I am to kiss you too.

*EARL and KRISTIN let themselves be kissed.*

CHARLIE: Dad, Kristin, this is Galina.

GALINA: Charlie is telling me many the anecdote of you. He says you are screaming with your arms when you are making love.

CHARLIE: Galina—

GALINA: This is true, you are screaming shout with arms when you are stewing? No, *screwing*. That is correct: *screwing*. This is true?

CHARLIE: Galina—stop!

GALINA: I am only wishing to put at ease. You have said all must relax for your big emission.

CHARLIE: Yeah, sure, but that doesn't mean—

*LUKE returns, followed by JULIE.*

LUKE: Here's a young lady I found wandering around basement number three.

CHARLIE: Julie! I knew you wouldn't let me down. I adore you! Hail, hail, the gang's all here. My whole family. I'm getting choked up. We're almost ready to start. We'll just ease into it. We'll chat about this and that, and the cameras will start filming, and I'll ask each of you some questions, and then you'll tell your stories. You must be totally relaxed. Everybody ready? Ready, Julie?

## 22. ANECDOTES

NARRATOR: They chat about this and that. The cameras start filming. Charlie's at the top of his game. Playful, amusing, intense, impassioned. Slowly but surely he persuades each of them to talk. Galina stands on a chair to act out a memorable event of her twentieth birthday. She was standing on top of a tall building in a high wind. Her scarf was blown off. She leaned over the railing to grab it. And she fell—four storeys.

Miraculously, she landed on a truckload of pillows. Nobody is sure that it really happened, but they love the anecdote anyway. It's spectacular, unique, extraordinary. Then Queenie begins a long, incomprehensible story, which Charlie translates into a very funny anecdote about one of Queenie's clients whom she saved from terminal depression by the daily application of a grapefruit facial. Then Earl and Kristin use sign language to describe their first meeting: how they spent the whole evening, one entire night, making love, without speaking a single word, and how Earl only figured out the next morning that Kristin was mute. Queenie keeps trying to interrupt, Kristin shouts with her arms, and Earl almost loses control, but then Charlie says, "Well, that's my family, honestly, authentically human." Julie listens to all of them, perfectly still. Then her brother turns to her.

CHARLIE: Your turn now, Julie. I remember, when you were little, how you loved looking at bugs.

*JULIE says nothing.*

When you were little, Julie . . .

*JULIE says nothing.*

GALINA: Go ahead, Julie. Share the little story you never told to anyone before. Yes, go. "When I was little . . . "

JULIE: When I was little . . .

CHARLIE: When you were little, you just stared at everything and everyone, right?

JULIE: When I was little . . . one day . . .

CHARLIE: One day . . . ?

JULIE: One day, in our living room . . .

CHARLIE: In our living room on Maple Street? What happened?

JULIE: Mom was demonstrating a new kind of makeup.

CHARLIE: Oh boy, Mom's demonstrations! Those were amazing. We should tell our viewers just how popular Mom was. There was an actual waiting list to attend her demonstrations. Who was there that night, do you remember?

JULIE: Mrs. Dutton, Mrs. Prince, Marjorie O'Dowd, and a bunch of others.

CHARLIE: What about me? I must've been around somewhere. I always was. I loved those demonstrations. It was like going to see a play. So, what happened?

JULIE: Mom handed out the free samples, and Mrs. Dutton said she'd like another one for her sister-in-law who couldn't be there that night, and Mrs. Tetley got so excited, she started right in, applying the makeup. But Mom said, "Wait now, Mary Beth, I must explain exactly how it's done."

CHARLIE: Meanwhile, Julie, what were you doing?

JULIE: I was sitting in the corner, as usual, behind the floor lamp, watching. Mom said, "Come sit with us, Julie. Come show the ladies your broken tooth. Julie broke a tooth this week. Come tell them how you did it. It's such a funny story." I thought, "What story?" For me, it wasn't a story, and I couldn't see anything very funny about breaking a tooth and then finding it in your chocolate bar. And, while I was thinking about this, my brother started to tell them about a big fat man he saw on the way home from school. The fat man leaned over to pick something up and he split the seat of his trousers. My brother acted the story out. He made the sound of the fat man's trousers splitting open, and everybody laughed.

CHARLIE: I always loved to make people laugh, that's true, but I honestly don't remember that particular—

JULIE: I knew the man's trousers couldn't have made that much noise, and that the man wasn't nearly as fat as my brother said, and that he was making most of it up. He kept imitating the sound, and Mom said, "Stop it, Charlie, you're going to make us die laughing," and Mrs. Dutton said, "Your son is amazingly talented. One day he'll be on the stage, just wait and see," and in my head I was shouting, "But it's not true, he's making it all up. He'd say anything, just to get you to look at him and clap for him and love him. But why? Why should we have to tell lies, in order to be loved?" And Marjorie O'Dowd opened her big mouth to tell about something strange she'd seen on the street, but my brother was already on to another, even funnier story, and without even thinking about it, I stood up, I held my arms like this, the left one stretched out straight, the right one folded, wrapped around the barrel, my hands gripping an automatic rifle—I squeezed the trigger and I fired. I fired into my brother's mouth, my mother's mouth, Mrs. O'Dowd's mouth, into all those chattering and laughing mouths, and it made this amazing noise, and it made my insides tremble as if the bullets were being fired from inside the deepest part of me, from somewhere deeper than me, and I watched their mouths explode, and the blood spurt out onto their skins and their clothes and the walls and the free samples of foundation makeup, and I ran out, I hid myself under the balcony, I cried and shook and threw up and didn't understand, I never understood the rifle fire which came out of me, and all the rage and all the fear and all the loneliness.

*A long silence.*

QUEENIE: What's he pay? What you bray, Mulie? You're petty. You're slick. What's a patter, baby cousin?

JULIE: Sorry, I-I have to phone, I've got a meeting, to catch my bus, my turn to cash out. They're waiting, somebody's waiting for me, some-where, for sure.

*JULIE stands and runs out.*

CHARLIE: Julie!

*A pause. CHARLIE regains his composure.*

I . . . So, there you go. That's how families are: ordinary people, with extraordinary stories.

*General uneasiness. KRISTIN speaks in sign language.*

EARL: She says it's a good time now for a moment of silence.

*Voices are heard, off. CHARLIE makes an effort to smile.*

CHARLIE: Oh! Wait now. What's that I hear? Yes, it's the chorus. It's your chorus, Mom. They wanted to surprise you. A big surprise just for you. Understand? Poof! They've been waiting outside. Let's go welcome them to the show.

NARRATOR: Charlie leads Queenie out to the hallway. The Word-Finders chorus comes in and sings, and Charlie remarks on how moving it is. Meanwhile, Julie is running through the hallways of basement number two of the big television studio. In her head, Charlie is shouting, "Julie! Come back!" She finds an escalator and runs up it, two steps at a time, then runs out the exit. She hurries across the busy street and onto a bus waiting at the corner. "Hey, you forgot to pay!" She scratches around in her purse and drops all her loose change into the box. She moves to the back. And there she is now, beside a dozing woman. Her face is burning. The streets are burning. She's burning with shame. She watches the city fly past. She hears her heart pounding. The bus moves on. Time passes. The driver shouts, "End of the line!" She gets out. She walks straight ahead. Time passes. She notices a commuter-train station and boards a train without noticing its destination. She pays and finds a seat. She watches the city, then the suburbs, fly past. Industrial parks, vast parking lots. She hears Galina: "One chance to change your life." Time passes. She looks out at the countryside now. Trees, fields, farmhouses, barns, tractors. She looks up at the sky, the clouds, the mountains in the distance. Time passes. The conductor shouts, "End of the line!" She gets out. She walks along a country road. Sheep on the hillside. She notices a path that winds across a field. She takes this. She hears her brother saying, "You sit in your silence, watching us, despising us." She hears her own voice, "My life doesn't want to be saved." Time passes. A lot of time. She goes on walking. She looks up. Suddenly, right in front of her, a path winds through the forest. A well-worn path. The light through the leaves. Birdsong. The smell of moss. The forest. She looks around. She thinks, "Where am I?" She thinks, "I'm lost." She takes the path. She winds through the forest. She notices a tree stump and sits down. She looks around. Time passes. She falls asleep. Time passes. A lot of time.

## 23. THIS IS THE PLACE

TIMOTHY: This is the place. For sure. Trees, bushes, the wild.
Returning to the earth.
Rotting among the dead leaves.
Like that poem I learned in high school.
How did it go?
"Move him into the sun—
Gently its touch awoke him once . . . "
You say to me: "To hell with poetry. You don't understand, Timothy.
To hell with the place. To hell with how you got here."
I know.
"Just do it."
I know, I know.
But I also have to choose.
You chose, didn't you?
Chose that day in January, during a blizzard.
A big windy space between two superhighways.
Chose to dig a trench in the snow.
To lie down in the trench.
Chose to shoot yourself in the mouth.
Was there a precise moment when you chose those things?
A moment when you said to yourself, "It's today."
You said to yourself, "Timothy will be waiting for me tonight, but that's too bad.
Too bad, because now's the time."

How did you know it was the time?
Did you receive some kind of signal?
What were you doing, just before?
Before you pulled the trigger?
Did you review our list?
"Ten good reasons to leave the world behind."
Did you count up to a hundred, or a thousand?
Did you say anything?
Did you say something to me?
Did you get the shakes?
You say to me: "Just do it, Timothy.
Shut up and do it.
It only takes a second."
Okay. I'll shut up.
You're right, there should be silence.
It's a ritual.
Three steps forward.
A moment of silence.
A quick glance up at the sky.
You say to me: "Shut up."
Okay.
I'm doing it.
You'll see.
I'm doing it.

TIMOTHY *takes a hunting rifle out of his gym bag.*

Three steps.
One, two, three.
A moment of silence.

TIMOTHY *sees* JULIE, *who appears from behind a tree.*

What the—? You— What do you—?

JULIE: Sorry. I didn't see you. I didn't know. I-I'm just passing through.

TIMOTHY: Okay.

*JULIE looks at the rifle TIMOTHY is holding.*

I'm hunting.

JULIE: Oh. Okay.

*Pause.*

Right. I-I think—somebody's expecting me.

TIMOTHY: Okay. Goodbye.

*JULIE starts out, then stops.*

What?

JULIE: Nothing. I was just wondering . . .

TIMOTHY: What?

JULIE: What are you hunting?

TIMOTHY: A wild animal.

JULIE: Oh.

*Pause.*

TIMOTHY: Okay then . . . Goodbye.

JULIE: Yes. Goodbye.

*JULIE takes a few more steps, then stops again.*

Do you come here often?

TIMOTHY: No. Never.

*Pause.*

JULIE: Did you come by bus?

TIMOTHY: No. I thumbed a ride.

JULIE: Oh. Me neither. I mean, I've never been here before. In fact, I don't even know where I am. Maybe that seems weird to you, but—

TIMOTHY: Listen, I-I don't really have time to—

JULIE: I understand. I didn't want to— Okay. I'm going.

*She leaves.* TIMOTHY *watches her disappear.*

TIMOTHY: Right.
Three steps forward.
One, two, three.

*Pause.*

Did you say something to me, just before?
Did you say, "Forgive me, Timothy"?
We took an oath.
Then you left me all alone.
How could you do that?
I know, this is no time for explanations.
I just have to *do* it.
A ritual.
A moment of silence.

*Pause.* JULIE *reappears.* TIMOTHY *is startled.*

JULIE: So you . . . You enjoy hunting?

TIMOTHY: Are you back again? What do you want?

JULIE: I've heard that—I read somewhere that people who enjoy hunting . . .

TIMOTHY: What?

JULIE: People who enjoy hunting don't like to eat meat. Or maybe the opposite. I don't remember. I'm always doing that—reading something and then not remembering. How about you?

TIMOTHY: Me?

JULIE: What do you think?

TIMOTHY: About what?

JULIE: About all that.

TIMOTHY: I don't know.

   *Pause.*

JULIE: Will you—will you eat your wild animal?

TIMOTHY: No. I won't.

JULIE: Oh. So you don't like meat. But do you like fish?

TIMOTHY: Look, I've got nothing to say about all that. I've got nothing to say about anything, okay?

JULIE: I don't either. But there's nothing wrong with that. The topic doesn't really matter. You can build on virtually anything. Are you planning to shoot it soon, your wild animal?

TIMOTHY: Yes. Soon.

JULIE: How will you do it?

TIMOTHY: By squeezing the trigger. Like this.

JULIE: What if it doesn't show up?

TIMOTHY: It'll show up.

JULIE: Your hands. Looks like you've got the shakes.

TIMOTHY: Listen, didn't I already say—?

JULIE: I know. You've got something to do. But wouldn't you like to talk about it? We could chat.

TIMOTHY: I don't care to.

JULIE: I don't care to either. I mean, it's difficult for me too. You can't imagine how difficult. I never care to, and I never know what to say, but you just have to dive in. You must focus on the other person. We're in this together. Don't forget, it takes both of us.

TIMOTHY: There is no "both of us." We are alone. You may think there are two of us, but we're born alone and we die alone.

JULIE: That's what I used to think, but—

TIMOTHY: Listen, if you'd just get out of here, I could get on with what I have to do, okay? Because now's the time. I'm feeling it.

JULIE: But wait. I-I'll tell you an anecdote. When I was little, I shot my brother and my mother in the mouth with an automatic rifle and there was an explosion and screaming and blood everywhere.

TIMOTHY: What?

JULIE: That may not be the whole truth, but that's what an anecdote is. You take a little piece of reality and you work on it, you reinvent it, so that it becomes surprising and fascinating.

*Pause.*

Earlier today I made a fool of myself on TV. That's not an anecdote, that's the truth.

*TIMOTHY prepares to fire the rifle.*

What are you doing?

TIMOTHY: She said to me, "You just don't have it." She wrote to me and said, "I always knew you didn't have it. It's not your fault. Some have got it and some don't." She wrote that on a postcard and sent it to me. I got it three days after.

JULIE: After what?

TIMOTHY: What do you think? You think I've got it?

JULIE: I don't know. Sure you do. I mean, we tell ourselves, "I don't have it," "I'm not capable," "I could never," but it's not true. We have more resources than we know. See? Just like now. We're talking. You say something to me and I reply, I keep it going. I ask you, uh . . . What was the picture on the postcard?

TIMOTHY: A moose.

JULIE: Well. That's interesting.

TIMOTHY: No, it's not. She probably bought it at the corner grocery. She just grabbed the one on top. She didn't give a shit.

JULIE: Well. That's strange. Me too, I often just grab the one on top.

TIMOTHY: Turn around.

JULIE: Why?

TIMOTHY: Turn around. Like this.

*He turns her around.*

Now, keep walking, okay? One hundred steps forward, without turning back. One hundred steps, understand?

JULIE: And what are you going to do?

TIMOTHY: I'm going to stay right here. Waiting for the wild animal. Off you go. One, two, three, four . . .

*He points the rifle at her.*

JULIE: Wait! I-I— How do you feel about anal sex?

TIMOTHY: Huh?

JULIE: And a girl's sex parts on your lips. Or her breasts in your face. Or—I don't know— She sits down on your chest, and maybe there's another girl behind her who—

TIMOTHY: Stop.

JULIE: Me, I'm not very— I mean, my sex life isn't very— Let's just say it's "modest," but, just the same, I've got ideas. For example: in the forest, at the foot of a tree. Naked on the ground, with your head on a pillow of moss, and, I don't know—with your legs spread wide, a breeze over your sex parts, and maybe a wild animal watching. I don't know why but I find that exciting: an animal watching. How about you? What do you like?

TIMOTHY: Nothing.

JULIE: That can't be. There must be some secret something which you've never shared with anybody.

*Pause. TIMOTHY lowers the rifle.*

TIMOTHY: I loved her breasts, her head, her spirit, her sex.

JULIE: Whose sex?

TIMOTHY: Rosalie's.

JULIE: That's a pretty name, Rosalie.

TIMOTHY: She thought it was stupid, a name from a fairy tale.

JULIE: I think I've got the wrong first name too.

TIMOTHY: The first time I saw her, I knew right away.

JULIE: That her name was Rosalie?

TIMOTHY: That she was only pretending. It was at a party. She was dancing all by herself in the middle of the room. The others probably thought, "She's just a girl, having a good time, taking a bite out of life." I was watching from across the room.

JULIE: Parties are the worst. I know. Sitting by yourself in the corner, holding your beer in both hands, swaying to the music so you don't look like a fool, and all you really want is to get out of there.

TIMOTHY: I didn't want to get out. I walked right up to her.

JULIE: You walked up to her with your heart pounding. I know. Connecting with someone at a party, it's the worst. You don't know whether the time is right. You try to think of something original to say.

TIMOTHY: I came up close to her and said, "We are the same."

JULIE: Nothing else?

TIMOTHY: "You and me, we pretend we're twenty-five. But, in fact, we're much older."

JULIE: You really said that?

TIMOTHY: It just came out. I felt like I'd been staring at her for a thousand years. I knew her phony energy by heart, the uneasiness in her eyes, the sickness which never left her.

JULIE: What sickness?

TIMOTHY: The sickness of disbelief, of feeling disgusted by the world, by other people, by everything. Sometimes so strong, sometimes just a dull ache which you deaden with beer or sex, but it never goes away.

JULIE: Like a toothache?

TIMOTHY: Sure. Maybe. A rotten tooth which was already there when you were born, imbedded deep in your gums. At first you try to pull it out, you use the big pliers, pull at it for all you're worth, but it does no good. Then one day you say to yourself, "I'll never be free of it."

JULIE: You fell in love with Rosalie?

TIMOTHY: "Love" is not the word. I became her and she became me.

JULIE: Like Siamese twins?

TIMOTHY: Yes. Attached to each other by that rotten tooth. You say to yourselves, "Deaden it for as long as you can, and, afterwards, get on with it, kill the sickness and then it'll all be over. Choose the right day, the right place, and just do it. Together."

JULIE: I don't understand.

TIMOTHY: We spent three years like that. Then one night she said, "You'll never do it, I know that. It's not your fault. You don't have it in you. Death. Some have got it and some don't." The next day she left early while I was still asleep. She went to the corner grocery and bought that ridiculous postcard. Mailed it to me. It was January. A blizzard. She lay down in the snow. And pulled the trigger. It was two days before they found her.

JULIE: She really shot herself?

TIMOTHY: She killed herself. All alone. I thought I'd die of the pain, but I didn't die. I cried, I drank, I smoked everything I could get my hands on, I walked all night, I slept around. Everybody told me, "You'll get over it." I didn't get over it. I bought this gun.

*Pause.*

JULIE: What's your name?

TIMOTHY: Timothy.

JULIE: I'm so sorry, Timothy.

TIMOTHY: No, you're not sorry. You don't know me, and you didn't know her.

JULIE: Pardon me. Excuse me. I'm looking for the right words, but it's hard.

TIMOTHY: I know. Go away now. Okay?

JULIE: No.

TIMOTHY: Why not?

JULIE: We haven't finished.

TIMOTHY: Finished what?

JULIE: Our conversation.

TIMOTHY: Please.

JULIE: We have to reach a conclusion. It's called the art of closure. Very important. Otherwise . . .

TIMOTHY: Otherwise what?

JULIE: Otherwise . . . I don't know. Otherwise, we'll have missed out on something, maybe. We've built something together and now we should complete it.

TIMOTHY: I haven't built anything. I'm here with this gun, that's all.

JULIE: But we did build something, just now. We're two people with no reason to meet one another in a forest, but we did meet one another, and we talked for a few minutes. Don't you see that as a miracle?

TIMOTHY: No, I don't see. I don't see anything.

*He takes up his gun again.*

Stay right where you are, okay? I don't know the art of closure, but I do know that this is almost over.

JULIE: Okay. But—

TIMOTHY: No.

JULIE: But promise me—when the wild animal arrives, when you've got it in your sights, think of a question that you could ask me.

TIMOTHY: What kind of question?

JULIE: I don't know. You could pick up on something I said, or on something you noticed about how I look. Whatever you like.

TIMOTHY: But I told you—

JULIE: Promise me.

TIMOTHY: Okay, I promise. But you also have to promise me.

JULIE: What?

TIMOTHY: Walk straight ahead. Don't come back. Whatever happens, don't come back here.

JULIE: That will be hard.

TIMOTHY: Just promise me.

JULIE: Okay. I promise.

TIMOTHY: Now go.

JULIE: I'm going. It was nice talking to you, Timothy.

TIMOTHY: Goodbye.

JULIE: "Nice" isn't the right word. It was interesting. No. Enlightening. No. Encouraging. Yes. It was encouraging.

TIMOTHY: Were you looking for courage?

JULIE: Very much.

TIMOTHY: Go on now.

*He gestures for her to go.*

JULIE: Okay. I'm going. Good luck, Timothy.

*She walks straight ahead, one hundred steps. She hears a rifle shot. She stops. She does not turn back.*

## 24. I BLEED IT SO

NARRATOR: Three months go by. After *Extraordinary Stories Of Ordinary People*, after the forest, the encounter, the rifle shot, the journey of hours to find the highway again, the night in a shabby motel, the next day's bus ride, the return home, the three days and nights without venturing outside, the following week's premiere telecast, with the automatic rifle and all the bloodshed edited out. Only the beginning of Julie's story remained, intercut with pictures of trees and ants, a weird unfinished story, and then back to work, lots of questions from her co-workers, lots of evasive answers. And now it's the end of summer, it's a Sunday, seven o'clock in the evening, at the entrance to a big park. In the distance, an open-air stage with rows of folding chairs in front of it.

*JULIE strides in. QUEENIE follows, but then stops.*

QUEENIE: I cook alight?

JULIE: Yes, Mom, you look lovely.

*QUEENIE touches her hair.*

QUEENIE: My fair? My fair's abovely?

JULIE: Your hair is lovely. You are beautiful.

QUEENIE: Not blue. You pay to bake me lappy.

JULIE: I say it because you're beautiful. Come on.

*GEORGE comes in.*

**GEORGE:** Oh, Deenie. Good, good. You look roughly. Bravo. The cress! I love it. Upstanding.

*He indicates her dress and gestures his approval.*

**QUEENIE:** Oh, that's lust battery.

**GEORGE:** No, no, no. You're a newel, a stork whining in the sty.

**QUEENIE:** Thanks a lot, but—

*GEORGE turns to JULIE.*

**GEORGE:** And you. I saw you at the telemission rudio. Facting like you had a nun. Mild stuff!

*He acts out picking up an automatic rifle and firing it.*

**JULIE:** I know, I know, you were at the studio and you saw what I did. I made myself ridiculous. Mom, it's time for you to get ready.

**GEORGE:** Were you slick? Sick?

**JULIE:** No, I wasn't sick. I'm a failure, that's all. Nothing has helped. Not the Internet, not the workshops, not counselling, not standing up straight, not speaking louder, not smiling sweetly, not accepting the void, not building my confidence, and not being myself. Nothing helps. Especially not being myself. That's just how it is. Just like you—you try to speak correctly, you throw yourself into it, you say things and you're sure you've found the right words, but you haven't. Not at all. And singing your songs together, that changes nothing. You think you can change. You encounter someone in the most unlikely place. You build something together, and it gives you hope for a few minutes, but afterwards it falls apart and you hear that rifle shot in your mind every single night. You try with all your might to carry on, but it just keeps falling apart. That is life. This fucking life of ours. Mine, at least.

*An uneasy silence.*

GEORGE: Notter you balking? I don't pet it. Not true. I was totally crocked out. Mild stuff. Rolled me right over.

*He acts out firing an automatic rifle several more times.*

JULIE: Okay, I get it. You were crocked out and rolled over. Except that's not the truth, and I know it's not.

*ANITA appears in the distance.*

ANITA: Queenie, George—come along! Everybody's here. We have to get ready. We start in half an hour.

GEORGE: Yeah, yeah, summing!

*He tries to take QUEENIE along.*

Don't you hear Rita?

*QUEENIE refuses to budge.*

QUEENIE: I'll sum, I'll hum. Go on. I hollow.

*She gestures for GEORGE to leave. He leaves. QUEENIE and JULIE are left alone.*

My Mulie. My earl. What's it? What's with new?

JULIE: Nothing. Nothing's new, Mom. But that's all right. That's just how it is.

*She tries to draw* QUEENIE *along, but* QUEENIE *pulls away and starts to talk very rapidly.*

QUEENIE: What's the new? What rakes you kraut? It fakes me heartlick to key you this day. And why'd you snoot us on the wee-tee? Snoot at Paulie and Beena and your bad and his shady and me. You snoot at *me*. My? Since you piddle, you sink I won't huv you. I shant outstand, blue enough, never outstood. But two can huv somedoddy though not outstanding. Expecially if that's your kotter and jazz such morrow keep in her wise. Sell me why you snoot. Sell me with your bands, with your harms, with fall to you. I bleed that. I bleed it so.

*QUEENIE hugs JULIE very tightly. JULIE holds her mother tightly too, but then pulls away.*

JULIE: Me too, Mom, I bleed it, I bleed it so. I'm not sure what you're trying to say, but I'm sure that I bleed it too.

QUEENIE: Sum. Hum with she.

*She tries to lead JULIE away.*

JULIE: No. You go ahead. I'm going for a little walk before it starts.

QUEENIE: You weave. You never give me for.

JULIE: Yes, I forgive. I'm just going for a little walk. I'll come back, I promise.

*She explains this with gestures and crosses her heart.*

## 25. CONVERSATION

NARRATOR: A little later, on a nearby street. Julie has walked around the block several times, her head full of her mother's confusion. She didn't know, she will never know for sure that Queenie was trying to say to her: "What's with you? What makes you shout? It makes me heartsick to see you this way. And why did you shoot at us on TV? Shoot at Charlie and Galina and your dad and his wife and me? You shot at *me*. Why? Since you were little, you've thought that I don't love you. I can't understand you, true enough, I never understood you. But you can love somebody without understanding. Especially if she's your own daughter and has such sorrow deep in her eyes. Tell me why you shot us. Tell me with your hands, with your arms, with all of you. I need that. I need it so."

> *JULIE walks up and down, lost in her thoughts. She suddenly bumps into someone. It's* TIMOTHY. *They stare at one another.*

TIMOTHY: Hello.

JULIE: Oh! Hello. You're not—I mean, you didn't—?

TIMOTHY: No, I didn't.

JULIE: Good. I was thinking. I thought—

TIMOTHY: You thought I had the courage.

JULIE: No. I wasn't thinking about courage.

TIMOTHY: I didn't have it. At the last minute I shifted my aim. I fired to one side. A few inches to one side of courage.

JULIE: I heard you. But I didn't come back.

TIMOTHY: I wanted to do it. With everything in me.

JULIE: Sometimes wanting to is not enough.

TIMOTHY: She was right: I haven't got it.

JULIE: Some have got it and some don't. That's how it is.

TIMOTHY: Well, look, I—I should be going.

JULIE: Okay, but . . . What's become of you?

TIMOTHY: I've become a guy who didn't commit suicide.

JULIE: Good. That's good. I should say, "That's cool."

TIMOTHY: You think so?

JULIE: Don't you?

TIMOTHY: I don't know. Depends on the day.

    *Pause.*

JULIE: But what do you—what do you do with yourself? I mean, in general. For work, for fun, and all that?

TIMOTHY: I tend bar for eight hours, I sleep for ten hours, and the rest of the time I walk.

JULIE: You walk?

TIMOTHY: If I stop walking, it all comes back.

JULIE: What comes back? The toothache?

TIMOTHY: The toothache, the pain, the shame, the feeling that I'll never succeed. Not at death and not at life either.

JULIE: I understand. Me too, I . . .

TIMOTHY: You too what?

JULIE: Me too, I have a rotten tooth.

TIMOTHY: Really? What do you do to make the pain go away? Sleep for ten hours, walk for eight hours?

JULIE: No, I seek out cancers for eight hours, I sleep for seven hours, and the rest of the time, I . . . I try to fit in, like working the eggs into the dough, but I don't ever succeed, and at night I do everything I can to avoid soliloquizing.

TIMOTHY: To avoid what?

JULIE: The temptations of solitude, you know? It's not easy. I slip up. And then, twice every week, I pretend to have a conversation with my mother. We don't understand each other, but at least it's a dialogue. And I read. And I think. I think a lot.

NARRATOR: While they talk, Julie and Timothy arrive back at the park where The Word-Finders are giving their concert.

*THE WORD-FINDERS can be heard, singing in the distance.*

JULIE: They've started! I should go. My mother's chorus is singing. I nearly forgot. Strange, how time passes when you're talking. I really have to go. I promised.

TIMOTHY: Okay. Well . . . Enjoy.

JULIE: They mess up all the words, it's pretty weird, but sometimes I find it moving, and my mother put on too much lip gloss, and my brother will be there, looking daggers at me, but his Russian lady friend will kiss me and tell me that he will forgive me, one of these days, and afterwards there's a party for everyone in the chorus and all their friends, with sandwiches and sickeningly sweet wine, and that will be the ultimate test, and I'll go on thinking about dying, but I won't die.

TIMOTHY: What would you die from?

JULIE: I can't explain. Not enough time. But do you think maybe . . . ?

TIMOTHY: What?

JULIE: Do you think maybe, one day, after my eight hours at the lab and before your eight hours at the bar, do you think we might continue our conversation, Timothy?

TIMOTHY: I . . . I don't know. I . . .

*THE WORD-FINDERS can be heard more clearly now.*

*ANITA is conducting them and singing:*

ANITA: "How can there be a cherry that has no stone?
How can there be a chicken that has no bone?
How can there be a ring that has no end?
How can there be a baby with no crying?"

*At the same time:*

THE WORD-FINDERS: "How can there be a Mary that has no phone?
How can she be a quicken that has no tone?
How can he be a sing that has to bend?
How can she see a table and go buying?"

JULIE: I already have so many more questions. They're building and building—here they come! Where do you tend bar? Where do you go walking for the rest of the day? What's your favourite beer? What did you do right after you shifted your aim a few inches to one side? Did you cry? Did you get the shakes? Did you throw up? What's your favourite bedtime snack? That day in the forest, just before you pulled the trigger, did you think of a question you might ask me? Do you have a brother but you're not sure if you really like him? And that day in the forest, is it possible that our conversation, the small thing which we built together for just a few minutes, do you think that might have saved your life? Could we at least consider it? Many more questions are coming to me, but forgive me for soliloquizing. It won't always be like that, I promise. You say something and then I'll say something. What do you say?

TIMOTHY: Small Talk.

JULIE: What?

TIMOTHY: "Small Talk," that's the name of the bar where I work. As in to talk about everything and about nothing. Like people do in a bar, get the idea?

JULIE: I get it.

TIMOTHY: A silly name. Not easy to remember.

JULIE: I'll remember.

*She starts towards the concert.*

TIMOTHY: Hey! What's your name?

JULIE: Is that what you thought about asking me, just before pulling the trigger?

TIMOTHY: It's what I'm asking you now.

JULIE: Julie.

TIMOTHY: Good luck, Julie!

NARRATOR: Julie mingles with the other concertgoers. Timothy goes on with his walk. The chorus goes on singing. And, of course, I sing along.

*Led by ANITA:*

**THE WORD-FINDERS & NARRATOR:**
"A cherry when it's blooming, it has no stone.
A chicken when it's pipping, it has no bone.
A ring when it's rolling, it has no end.
And a baby when it's sleeping has no crying."

*End.*

## ACKNOWLEDGEMENTS

The playwright wishes to thank Le Centre des auteurs dramatiques, and Elizabeth Bourget in particular, for support provided at various stages in the writing of this play. Thanks also to all actors who participated in workshops of the text.

Carole Fréchette was born in Montréal and is a graduate of the National Theatre School. She is the author of fifteen plays, which have been translated into twenty languages and staged all over the world. Fréchette was awarded the prestigious Siminovitch Prize in Theatre in 2002, and has received the Governor General's Literary Award for French Language Drama twice, for *Le Quatre Morts de Marie* in 1995 and for *Small Talk* in 2014. Her plays are published in French by Leméac/Actes-Sud Papiers.

John Murrell is one of Canada's most frequently produced playwrights, whose work has been translated into numerous languages and presented throughout the world. He is also a translator of Chekhov and Ibsen, among others, and of eight plays by Carole Fréchette, all of which have been published by Playwrights Canada Press. Murrell is an Officer of the Order of Canada and a recipient of the Governor General's Performing Arts Award for Lifetime Artistic Achievement.

First edition: September 2018
Printed and bound in Canada by Imprimerie Gauvin, Gatineau

Photo of Carole Fréchette © Claude Dolbec

PLAYWRIGHTS
CANADA PRESS

202-269 Richmond St. W.
Toronto, ON
M5V 1X1

416.703.0013
info@playwrightscanada.com
www.playwrightscanada.com
@playcanpress

MIX
Paper from
responsible sources
FSC® C100212